#Houst(

Apollo 11 - When Men Walked on the Moon

By Philip Gibson

What if there had been social media during the first mission to land a man on the Moon in 1969?

If you were not fortunate enough to be able to witness the entire historic mission as it unfolded, this account will put you believably back inside those eight incredibly tense and dramatic days. The unique social media format of the book allows us to experience all the drama and achievements as if we were following them live, and as if the participants were speaking to us directly in real time. The narrative is based on actual astronaut accounts, NASA transcripts of the fascinating continual communications with the astronauts, broadcasts of the all main TV networks covering the mission and the thoughts of many laypeople observers. The account also includes details that were not publically available at the time, such as the secret speech to be delivered by President Nixon should the astronauts fail to return from the Moon. There is an extensive list of major sources at the end of the book.

It is not a book, therefore, written in the usual book format. It is the story of man's first exploration of Earth's nearest neighbor, the Moon, told as if in real time in the form of imaginary social media posts by the main participants and observers. Although using the fictional (at the time) vehicle of social media, the book gives an accurate account of the historic mission, revealing what the people involved in, and those witnessing, the momentous events were thinking, doing and saying at each stage of the mission.

The account covers the entire mission, from the tense build up and countdown to the launch to the heart-stopping descent to the lunar surface, the first moonwalk, the experiments on the surface, the journey back to Earth, re-entry, recovery and the triumphal reception back in New York.

Walter Cronkite (1916-2009)

Walter Cronkite was best known as the main anchorman for the American CBS television news network during much of the Cold War in the 1950s, 1960s and 1970s. Often referred to as "the most trusted man in America", Cronkite was the face of American news during the Cuban Missile Crisis, the assassinations of Martin Luther King, John F. Kennedy and Robert Kennedy; throughout the American space program, Moon landings and the war in Vietnam.

Launch Day

Walter Cronkite @WCCBSNews
Just hours to go now before the launch of Apollo 11 and we have learned that President Nixon's pre-launch dinner with the astronauts yesterday was cancelled. It seems that even presidents have germs, and the NASA doctors didn't want to risk it.

Walter Cronkite @WCCBSNews
The astronauts, the prime crew, were wakened at 4.15 a.m. Eastern Daylight Time this morning. They then underwent a thorough physical examination, after which they were declared 'flight ready'.

Walter Cronkite @WCCBSNews
They then sat down for the normal astronaut fare on launch day of orange juice, steak, scrambled eggs, toast and coffee. They were joined by two of their colleagues: Director of Flight Crew Operations Deke Slayton and back up command module pilot Bill Anders.

Walter Cronkite @WCCBSNews
The astronauts departed from their crew quarters, after checking out their suits, at 6.27 a.m., and some 27 minutes later, 8 miles away atop the launch pad, the commander astronaut Neil Armstrong was the first to board the spacecraft.

Neil Armstrong (1930 - 2012)

Neil Armstrong was a naval aviator, test pilot, aerospace engineer, and university professor. Before becoming an astronaut, Armstrong was an officer in the U.S. Navy and served in the Korean War.

After the war, he earned his bachelor's degree at Purdue University and served as a test pilot at the National Advisory Committee for Aeronautics High-Speed Flight Station. He later completed graduate studies at the University of Southern California. He made his first space flight, as command pilot of Gemini 8, in 1966, becoming NASA's first civilian astronaut to fly in space. On this mission, he performed the first docking of two spacecraft.

As spacecraft commander for Apollo 11, the first manned lunar landing mission, Armstrong gained the distinction of being the first man to land a craft on the Moon and first to step on its surface.

Edwin Eugene (Buzz) Aldrin (1930 -   )

Buzz Aldrin received a bachelor of science degree in 1951 from the United States Military Academy at West Point, New York, graduating third in his class. He has a doctorate of science in Astronautics from Massachusetts Institute of Technology, Cambridge. His thesis was "Guidance for Manned Orbital Rendezvous." Prior to joining NASA, Aldrin flew 66 combat missions in F-86's while on duty in Korea. Aldrin was one of the third group of astronauts named by NASA in October 1963.

On November 11, 1966, he and command pilot James Lovell were launched into space in the Gemini 12 spacecraft on a 4-day flight, which brought the Gemini program to a successful close. Aldrin established a new record for extravehicular activity (EVA), spending 5-1/2 hours outside the spacecraft. He served as lunar module pilot for Apollo 11, July 16-24, 1969, the first manned lunar landing mission. Aldrin followed Neil Armstrong onto the lunar surface on July 20, 1969, completing a 2-hour and 15 minute lunar EVA.

Since retiring from NASA, the Air Force, and his position as commander of the USAF Test Pilot School at Edwards Air Force Base in 1972, he has authored several books including the autobiography, "Return to Earth". He has remained at the forefront of efforts to ensure a continued leading role for America in manned space exploration to advance his life-long commitment to venturing outward in space.

Michael Collins (1930 -   )

Michael Collins received a Bachelor of Science degree from the United States Military Academy at West Point, New York, in 1952. He chose an Air Force career following graduation from West Point and served as an experimental flight test officer at the Air Force Flight Test Center, Edwards Air Force Base, California. In that capacity, he tested performance and stability and control characteristics of Air Force aircraft - primarily jet fighters.

Collins was one of the third group of astronauts named by NASA in October 1963 and served as backup pilot for the Gemini VII mission.

Collins served as command module pilot on Apollo 11, July 16-24, 1969 - the first lunar landing mission. He remained aboard the command module, Columbia, on station in lunar orbit while Neil Armstrong, spacecraft commander, and Edwin Aldrin, lunar module pilot, descended to the Moon's surface in their lunar module Eagle. Collins completed two space flights, logging 266 hours in space - of which 1 hour and 27 minutes were spent in EVA.

Walter Cronkite @WCCBSNews
A couple of days ago, we had our last close up look around the massive vessel that will surely rank in history with...perhaps Lindbergh's Spirit of St. Louis, Darwin's Beagle and Columbus's Santa Maria.

Walter Cronkite @WCCBSNews
How can a country which seems to have difficulty building a reliable washing machine build all these incredibly efficient space vehicles? Well, the answer lies in NASA's system of quality control.

Walter Cronkite @WCCBSNews
If American automobiles were built to the same quality control standards of, for example the lunar module, the price would be considerably higher. But then... so would the trade-in value.

David Brinkley @DBNBCNews
In Mission Control, Houston and in the Firing Room at Cape Kennedy, the atmosphere is as cool and quiet as if all those computers down there were figuring out a factory payroll.

Philip Gibson @philiplaos
American TV says 1 million people will be on site watching the launch. There will be hundreds of

millions more watching on TV. I'm so excited to be one of them even though I'm thousands of miles away on the other side of the Atlantic Ocean.

David Brinkley @DBNBCNews
This will be the most carefully planned, meticulously-engineered trip anywhere in the history of the world. In fact, probably the most carefully engineered ANYTHING in the history of the world.

Jack King @JKLaunchControl
We encountered a leaking valve in part of the equipment that is used to replenish the hydrogen fuel supply in the third stage of the Saturn V launch vehicle.

Jack King @JKLaunchControl
A team of technicians was sent out to the launch pad at about the time the astronauts were travelling to the pad. They tightened some bolts and we were able to bypass that valve and proceed with the countdown.

Walter Cronkite @WCCBSNews
While the Apollo 11 team prepare for lift off, there has been much speculation in recent days that the Soviets may be about to attempt some kind of Moon launch themselves.

Walter Cronkite @WCCBSNews
This race to the Moon has indeed been that – a race between the Soviet Union and the United States. It has been that way since the launch of the first Earth satellite and the first man into space by the Soviets.

Walter Cronkite @WCCBSNews
As always, a great deal of secrecy surrounds the intentions of the Soviet space program. It may, or

may not be, that their upcoming Moon mission (whatever it is) is intended to steal some of the glory from the Apollo 11 mission.

Philip Gibson (1950 -   )

I am a 63-year-old teacher of English and author of some 30+ books on ESL and History. During the Apollo 11 mission in 1969, I watched with growing interest the live TV broadcasts from American TV beamed into TV room in the holiday camp in southern England where I was working at a summer job in the fish and chip shop there. Forty-five years later, out of a sense of nostalgia and disappointment that no further manned missions beyond Earth orbit have been undertaken since the Apollo program, I sat down and started to do the extensive research for this book.

I hope you will enjoy reading it as much as I have enjoyed researching and writing it.

Philip Gibson @philiplaos
I just watched a simulation of the entire mission from launch to Moon landing to return to Earth. It astonishes me that they think they can pull this off! What incredible confidence and courage those NASA teams have.

David Brinkley @DBNBCNews
A small group of black activists are protesting that while billions are spent on the race to the Moon, not enough is spent on the hungry of this planet or this nation. In the shadow of a model of the lunar module, they held a small demonstration.

Rev. Ralph Albernathy @RevRalph
While wishing the astronauts a safe flight, we are here to say that what we can do for space and exploration, we MUST do, and we DEMAND that we do, the same thing for starving, poor people.

David Brinkley @DBNBCNews
We put the reverend's concern to the top NASA official who showed some sympathy with the protesters' point of view.

Thomas Payne (1921-1992)

Thomas Payne was an American scientist, administrator and manager. He had been tasked with getting the Apollo program back on track after the Apollo 1 disaster and was the most senior NASA administrator during the Apollo 11 Moon landing and several other Apollo missions including Apollo 13. He was also involved in preparing plans for the post-Apollo era, including plans for establishing a lunar base and a manned mission to Mars by 1981. However, those plans were never taken up by the political leadership in Washington.

Dr. Thomas Payne @TPayneNASA
If by not sending Apollo 11 to the Moon, I could wipe out poverty in America, I would not push the 'launch button'. But the button WILL be pushed. And it will be pushed at 9.32 a.m. Eastern Time if all goes well in the countdown.

David Brinkley @DBNBCNews
The walk on the Moon will probably be seen by more people around the world than have ever seen... anything. Perhaps more than a billion people worldwide.

David Brinkley @DBNBCNews
The countdown to lift off continues. So far, there has hardly been any delay at all.

David Brinkley @DBNBCNews
This whole area down here in the Florida Flats is filling up with perhaps a million people, all excited to watch the launch and to have something monumental to tell their grandchildren about.

David Brinkley @DBNBCNews
The hundreds of thousands of people out there are in tents, sleeping bags, campers and trailers. They are building fires at night and cooking hot dogs, playing guitars, transistor radios and drinking a little beer.

David Brinkley @DBNBCNews
One liqueur store on the beach nearby reported, happily, that they are selling 150 cases of beer a day.

David Brinkley @DBNBCNews
9.32 is the time... the time when those three men will leave Earth to take a walk on the Moon. It is impossible to believe... but it's true – those men are going to the Moon!

Eric Sevareid @ESCBSNews
After 9 years of preparation and 24 billion dollars spent, this, perhaps the greatest of man's exploration journeys is about to begin.

Eric Sevareid @ESCBSNews
Lindbergh, Glenn and now in all probability
Armstrong; these three will stand as the supreme
American heroes of the age. All three were raised as
boys in small mid-western towns. Armstrong remains
essentially a loner: inner-directed, as were Lindberg
and John Glenn.

Eric Sevareid @ESCBSNews
Perhaps there is something in the mystique of the
small American town and its formative influences.
They had security, they had leisure to prowl and to
dream. Innocence existed. Sophisticated tensions did
not press upon them.

Eric Sevareid @ESCBSNews
Intellectuals of literary bent seem disappointed that
their speech does not match the eloquence of their
achievement. But it is the silent artists like these three
men, the men who see beauty in the machinery and
its functions, who do these things.

Eric Sevareid @ESCBSNews
Artists they are because they are perfectionists
seeking the outer limits of their strengths and their
talents. Were they men of words, with their minds full
of poetic imagery or philosophical abstractions as they
fly, they would surely fail.

Philip Gibson @philiplaos
Eric Sevareid loves to wax poetical. I much prefer
Walter Cronkite's more down-to-Earth commentary. I
loved watching his features on the launch site, the
construction of the lunar module and the mobile
quarantine facility for the returning astronauts.

Philip Gibson @philiplaos
Also his description of the Moon rock examining laboratory and the Goldstone signal relay station. Walter Cronkite describes technical stuff so beautifully and clearly. He is a true poet of the technological age.

Walter Cronkite @WCCBSNews
Upon return to Earth, the Apollo 11 astronauts will spend 3 weeks in a portable quarantine trailer. They will enter the trailer immediately upon landing on the recovery ship.

Walter Cronkite @WCCBSNews
The mobile quarantine facility will be unloaded from USS Hornet in Hawaii and flown to Houston with the astronauts still inside.

Walter Cronkite @WCCBSNews
This procedure is undertaken because of the unlikely chance of a harmful organism travelling back with the astronauts to plague the Earth.

Dr. Martin Alexander @DRDMCornell
In my capacity as a soil bacteria scientist, I have examined NASA's quarantine procedures and conclude that they are far from adequate.

Dr. Martin Alexander @DRDMCornell
A much better and longer quarantine would provide more of a guarantee against the introduction to Earth of harmful invasive lunar bacteria.

Walter Cronkite @WCCBSNews
It is now T minus one hour 29 minutes, 53 seconds and counting. Just an hour and a half, if all goes well, to the launch of Apollo 11 on its mission to land a man on the Moon.

Walter Cronkite @WCCBSNews
If all does go well, astronauts Armstrong, Aldrin and Collins are to lift off from Pad 39-A on the voyage man has always dreamed about. Next stop for them… the Moon.

Walter Cronkite @WCCBSNews
The astronauts are on board now. They are strapped into their spacecraft atop the Saturn rocket third stage. They've been there for just about an hour, going through the final checkout of all the systems aboard the spacecraft.

Walter Cronkite @WCCBSNews
At 9.32 a.m. Eastern Time, that huge, 36-storey-high launch vehicle will thunder into life, pushing the astronauts into temporary orbit around the Earth. There are 9 million parts in the rocket itself and they all have to work perfectly during lift off.

Walter Cronkite @WCCBSNews
Two and a half hours after lift off, another rocket burn will send the spacecraft on its way to the Moon. And then on Sunday afternoon… the landing on the Moon.

Walter Cronkite @WCCBSNews
At 2.20 a.m., Monday, July 21st. – a date that will live will live in history as long as man is on this planet, or any other planet, 38-year-old Neil Alden Armstrong will become the first human being to touch the Moon.

Walter Cronkite @WCCBSNews
Aldrin will follow just 20 minutes later. And over the years to come, many others will walk on the desolate lunar surface. But Armstrong will take that first step… in more ways than one.

Walter Cronkite @WCCBSNews
Many things will never be the same again. For in addition to the many things the three astronauts will undertake, the experiments they will perform and the samples they will collect, these men will carry with them many other things.

Walter Cronkite @WCCBSNews
They will carry with them many things not nearly so easy to describe. There is the spirit of such men as Marco Polo, Columbus and Lindbergh.

Walter Cronkite @WCCBSNews
They will carry the dreams of Jules Verne and H.G. Wells, the vision of Kepler and Galileo, and the skill and courage of Shepherd, Glenn, Schirra, Gagarin, Titov and all the others.

Walter Cronkite @WCCBSNews
They will carry thoughts of Moon Goddess Diana, and, I suppose... of green cheese.

Walter Cronkite @WCCBSNews
And boring through the vastness, blackness and cold of space for just over 8 days, they will carry the pledge of President John F. Kennedy - to put a man on the Moon and bring him back safely to Earth, and to do it in this decade.

Walter Cronkite @WCCBSNews
And, it almost goes without saying, these brave astronauts will carry the dreams and hopes of all mankind on their shoulders.

Eric Sevareid @ESCBSNews
These astronauts are the men of Apollo 11 by the luck of the draw. But Armstrong will be the one to put the

first foot down on the Moon by somebody's deliberate decision.

Eric Sevareid @ESCBSNews
It is the logical suspicion that Armstrong is the chosen one, not only by reason of his undoubted competence, but also by reason of his personality and appearance.

Eric Sevareid @ESCBSNews
If the mission succeeds, this man will become THE symbolic American to the world. He fits the stereotype of the all-American boy, the kid next door, he has all his hair, he has French blue eyes, the smile of a slightly-shy young American man.

Philip Gibson @philiplaos
I think Eric Sevareid is competing with Walter Cronkite to provide the most erudite, philosophical coverage of this mission. If so, I believe Cronkite will win the competition hands down.

Walter Cronkite @WCCBSNews
There are thousands of VIP.s here to watch the launch. In fact, the protocol here got so difficult that NASA had to work up to VVIPs and finally worked up to VVVIPs – that's "very, very, very important persons".

Walter Cronkite @WCCBSNews
One VIP who has declined to come down to the launch is the Soviet ambassador. That is believed to be because if he came here, then the Soviets would be obliged to invite us to witness one of their launches.

Walter Cronkite @WCCBSNews
To have U.S. representatives witness a Soviet launch would of course be impossible given the secrecy about

the Soviet space program. One of the differences in the two programs is that the U.S. program is carried out, not in secret, but in the full glare of worldwide publicity.

Ike Samford @ISCBSNews
I am in the VIP area. It is divided into various sections. They designate VIPs, VVIPs, triple VIs, quadruple VIPs and so forth. Part of the stand is reserved for Vice-President Agnew and former President Johnson who has yet to arrive.

Ike Samford @ISCBSNews
There are 400 congressmen here as well as members of the Supreme Court. Also the presidential cabinet, 20 governors, 40 mayors and representatives of 60 nations.

Walter Cronkite @WCCBSNews
It is now 1 hour 18 minutes and 24 seconds to lift off of Apollo 11. We are watching the liquid hydrogen and liquid oxygen venting off into steam in the 85 degree heat here on the Florida coast.

Walter Cronkite @WCCBSNews
We now see former President Johnson taking his seat in the viewing stand along with Mrs. Johnson. The former president has been instrumental in getting the space program going.

Walter Cronkite @WCCBSNews
As senator, Johnson shared the burden of getting the first appropriations through. As vice-president, he was head of Kennedy's space council – a job he asked for, and Kennedy had to get the law changed to be able to give him the job.

Walter Cronkite @WCCBSNews
Lyndon Johnson has ridden along figuratively speaking in every one of the flights leading up to this point. He pushed the program through for a landing this decade against objections within the Administration itself. And now he is here to hopefully witness the culmination of all his efforts.

Walter Cronkite @WCCBSNews
We are now at 1 hour 4 minutes 25 seconds and counting to the launch of Apollo 11 to send men to the Moon and hopefully land there for the first time – a great adventure!

Walter Cronkite @WCCBSNews
All systems are checking out. The recovery vessels are waiting at their assigned points. The mission tracking stations are alert and ready. The radar is ready to lock on and follow the spacecraft in this massive effort.

Walter Cronkite @WCCBSNews
The flight of Apollo 11 is to be the culmination of a national effort to fulfill that goal set 8 years ago by John Kennedy. It is the most difficult and most dangerous mission mankind has so far attempted.

Jack King @JKLaunchControl
We've just passed the 56 minute mark in our countdown. We're still proceeding in an excellent manner at this time. All elements are reporting in that all systems are continuing to look good at this point.

Walter Cronkite @WCCBSNews
Great quality control is the name of the game in building these things. Of the nearly 9 million parts in

the Saturn rocket and the command module, each one has to work perfectly in unison with all the others.

Walter Cronkite @WCCBSNews
If you had just 100th of 1% of those parts fail, you'd have 9,000 parts not working. It's incredible the accuracy with which these things have to be put together. We are now at 53 minutes and counting to the launch of Apollo 11.

Jack King @JKLaunchControl
We are still aiming toward a planned launch at the start of the lunar window – 9.32 a.m. Eastern Daylight Time.

Jack King @JKLaunchControl
We have passed the 51 minute mark in our countdown. We are now at T minus 50 minutes 51 seconds and counting. Apollo 11 is still GO at this time.

Jack King @JKLaunchControl
In about 30 seconds, that big swing arm, that has been attached to the spacecraft up to now, will be moved back to a parked position some 5 feet away from the spacecraft. We will alert the astronauts because there is a little jolt when the swing arm is moved away.

Jack King @JKLaunchControl
Mark!... The swing arm is now coming back from the spacecraft. We have completed our telemetry checks with the launch vehicle, and at this point, with the swing arm back, we are arming the pyrotechnics.

Jack King @JKLaunchControl
The pyrotechnics are so the escape tower at the top of the spacecraft could be used if a catastrophic condition was going to occur under the astronauts with the launch vehicle.

Jack King @JKLaunchControl
We have the high-speed elevator located at the 320-foot level in the event the astronauts have to get out in a hurry. This is a special precaution for the astronauts' safety during the final stages of the countdown.

Jack King @JKLaunchControl
Astronaut Buzz Aldrin in the middle seat is working on setting up proper switch settings in preparation for pressurizing the reaction control system. These are the 16 thrusters, in 4 quadrants, around the service module which are used for maneuvers in space.

Walter Cronkite @WCCBSNews
We are hearing that Apollo 11 commander Neil Armstrong has been informed that the launch procedure is going so well that some aspects of the procedure are running 15 minutes ahead of schedule.

Walter Cronkite @WCCBSNews
Apparently, Armstrong answered, "That's fine – just as long as we don't launch 15 minutes early."

Walter Cronkite @WCCBSNews
Armstrong was referring, of course, to the 'launch window' which doesn't open until 9.32 a.m. Those windows are terribly important. The whole timeline of arrival at the Moon, the delicate operation of lunar descent, etc. all depend on incredibly precise timing throughout the mission.

Jack King @JKLaunchControl
The launch vehicle people are keeping a close eye on the propellant status on the spacecraft. Reports are that the propellants are stable. We keep an eye on these aspects throughout the count and use the aid of computers to keep an overall check on general status.

Jack King (1931 -   )

Jack King joined NASA in 1960 and was the Head of Public Information and Public Affairs officer during much of the NASA space program, including during the Mercury, Gemini and Apollo missions. His dramatic and technically-detailed commentary during the countdown to lift off of Apollo 11 has become the stuff of historic folklore of the modern age.

Jack King @JKLaunchControl
At lift off, we will have a vehicle weighing close to six and half million pounds on the launch pad, with more than a million gallons of propellant aboard the 3 stages of the spacecraft. We are now at T minus 44 minutes 21 seconds and counting.

Jack King @JKLaunchControl
Coming up shortly will be a key test here in the firing room – some final checks of the destruct system aboard the 3 stages on the Saturn V launch vehicle.

Jack King @JKLaunchControl
In the event, during early powered flight, that the vehicle strays rather violently off course, the safety officer could take action to destroy the vehicle.

Jack King @JKLaunchControl
Destruction of the vehicle obviously would occur after the astronauts have separated by their escape tower from the faulty vehicle.

Jack King @JKLaunchControl
All aspects of the mission remain GO at this time. We are at 39 minutes 47 seconds and counting.

Jack King @JKLaunchControl
We have passed the 36 minute mark in our countdown and have completed those safety command checks. The status report will now pass to Mission Control, Houston.

Clifford E. Charlesworth @CliffFlgtApollo11
We are ready to assume control of this flight when the Saturn V has cleared the tower.

Jack King @JKLaunchControl
We have just passed the 31-minute mark in our count at T minus 30 minutes 52 seconds and counting. We have completed checking out the various batteries in the 3 stages and instrument units in the Saturn V rocket.

Jack King @JKLaunchControl
We remain on external power through most of the countdown to preserve those batteries which must be used during the powered flight. We just take a look at them by going INTERNAL and then go EXTERNAL again.

Jack King @JKLaunchControl
The batteries all look good. The next time we go INTERNAL will be at the 57-second mark, and then the spacecraft will of course remain on internal power during the flight.

Jack King @JKLaunchControl
For the next 20 minutes, we will look at the systems inside the lunar module, then power down the telemetry at the 10-minute mark to preserve the power of the lunar module.

Jack King @JKLaunchControl
The lunar module of Apollo 11 when it separates from the command module, will have the call sign 'Eagle'. The command module call sign will be 'Columbia'.

Jack King @JKLaunchControl
We have just passed the 26 minute mark in the countdown. The Saturn V rocket and command module and lunar modules Columbia and Eagle are GO at this time.

Jack King @JKLaunchControl
We are now less than 16 minutes away from the planned lift off of Apollo 11. All is still going well with the countdown at this time. We have been performing final checks with the tracking beacons and the instrument unit.

Jack King @JKLaunchControl
When we get to the 3-minute 10 second mark in the countdown, we'll go on an automatic sequence. As far as the launch vehicle is concerned, all aspects from there on down will be automatic, run by the ground master computer here in the firing room.

Jack King @JKLaunchControl
At the 8.9 second mark in the countdown, the ignition sequence will begin in those 5 engines of the first stage of the Saturn V. At the 2 second mark, we'll get information and a signal that all engines are running.

Jack King @JKLaunchControl
At the zero mark in the countdown, once we get the commit signal – the signal that says the thrust is proper and acceptable - we will then get a commit and lift off as the hold-on arms release the vehicle.

Jack King @JKLaunchControl
We will have some 7.6 million pounds of thrust pushing the vehicle upwards – a vehicle that weighs close to 6.5 million pounds. We are now at 14 minutes 13 seconds and counting.

Jack King @JKLaunchControl
We have passed the 11-minute mark and are now at T minus 10 minutes 54 seconds. All is still GO at this time. The commander, Neil Armstrong, has performed

some final switch settings for the stabilization and control systems of the spacecraft.

Jack King @JKLaunchControl
The spacecraft is now on full internal power - on the full power of its fuel cells. Up to this time, it has been sharing the load with an external power source.

Walter Cronkite @WCCBSNews
Here at Kennedy Space Center waiting for the launch of Apollo 11, I'm sitting next to famed science fiction writer Arthur C. Clarke, the writer of so many works that were way ahead of the science of the time, including the wonderful 2001: A Space Odyssey.

Walter Cronkite @WCCBSNews
Arthur first wrote about a trip to the Moon back in 1930 at a time when nobody thought it would come this soon.

Arthur C. Clarke @ArthurC.Clarke
Back in 1930, I didn't imagine a manned Moon mission would take place in my lifetime. But now that it has, I'm already excitedly thinking about the next stage – Mars and beyond.

Arthur C. Clarke @ArthurC.Clarke
Regarding the Moon mission, I was right on many of the technical details. However, I never imagined the scale, the cost and the sheer complexity of what would be involved. If I had, I think I would have been discouraged.

Arthur C. Clarke @ArthurC.Clarke
I thought the whole thing would be acco
cost of a few million dollars.

Walter Cronkite @WCCBSNews
We are told that the cost of just this launch today alone is 69 million dollars, and many billions of dollars for the entire Apollo, Gemini and Mercury programs.

Arthur C. Clarke @ArthurC.Clarke
All this money is going to come back many times over in the generations to come. This is one of the best investments the United States has ever made. In 10 years, 20 years, people will wonder how we ever questioned this expenditure.

Walter Cronkite @WCCBSNews
I asked Arthur C. Clarke if he would like to tell me what his book and the later movie 2001 is all about. He declined, saying he didn't think we had time, what with this upcoming historic launch and what not... Oh, well.

Walter Cronkite @WCCBSNews
I expect to be seeing Arthur C. Clarke many times during the duration of this mission and he has just promised that, during quiet periods, he will explain to me the meaning of the black obelisk in 2001... I think I've got something there!

Jack King @JKLaunchControl
Both Armstrong and lunar module pilot Buzz Aldrin have now armed their rotational hand controllers – the controllers they will use in flight.

Jack King @JKLaunchControl
We have now gone to the automatic systems with the emergency detection system – the system that would ꭐe the astronauts if there's trouble down below with Saturn V rocket during powered flight.

Jack King @JKLaunchControl
We are now coming up on the 10-minute mark. Ten minutes away from our planned lift off of Apollo 11. T minus 10 minutes and we are still aiming for our planned lift off at 32 minutes past the hour.

Philip Gibson @philiplaos
I can see Former President Johnson on TV wiping the sweat from his forehead. I think I'm sweating watching this from here in England, not Florida... and it's not even warm here!

Jack King @JKLaunchControl
The spacecraft test conductor has now completed his check of his personnel in the control room. All report they are GO for the mission and this has been reported to the test supervisor Bill Schick.

Jack King @JKLaunchControl
We are now at 5 minutes 20 seconds and counting.

Jack King @JKLaunchControl
The lunar module telemetry has been powered down. We took a good look at Eagle and it looks good. The spacecraft test conductor for the lunar module reported that Eagle is GO.

Jack King @JKLaunchControl
The swing arm is now coming back to its fully-retracted position as our countdown continues. The astronauts have been informed. T minus 4 minutes 50 seconds and counting.

Jack King @JKLaunchControl
The astronauts will have a few more reports coming up in the countdown. The last business report will be

from Neil Armstrong at the 45 second mark in the count when he gives us status on the final alignment on the stabilization and control system.

Jack King @JKLaunchControl
We are now passing the 4 minute 30 second mark in the countdown, and we are still GO for Apollo 11 at this time. We will go on an automatic sequence starting at 3 minutes and 7 seconds.

Walter Cronkite @WCCBSNews
The engines that generate the necessary thrust at lift off have a combined horsepower equal to 543 jet fighter planes. The launch vehicle there weighs as much as the nuclear submarine Nautilus.

Walter Cronkite @WCCBSNews
The launch vehicle will burn over 5 million pounds of fuel – the equivalent of 98 railroad cars full of it, the capacity of a small town's entire water capacity.

Walter Cronkite @WCCBSNews
At lift off, the noise level reaches 120 decibels – which has been compared to 8 million hi-fi's all playing at once.

Clifford E. Charlesworth @CliffFlgtApollo11
I have polled the room and all flight directors report that Apollo 11 is GO for launch.

Jack King @JKLaunchControl
The final abort checks between several key members of the team here in the control center and the astronauts have now been completed. Launch Operations Manager Paul Donnelly wished the crew on the launch team's behalf, "Good luck and God speed!"

Jack King @JKLaunchControl
Three minutes 25 seconds and counting. We are still GO at this time. We will be coming up on the automatic sequence in 15 seconds. All is still GO at this time.

Jack King @JKLaunchControl
Neil Armstrong reported back when he received the good wishes, "Thank you very much. We know it will be a good flight."

Jack King @JKLaunchControl
Firing command is coming in now. We are on the automatic sequence, approaching the 3-minute mark in the count. T minus 3 minutes. We are GO with all elements of the mission at this time.

Jack King @JKLaunchControl
We are on an automatic sequence as the master computer supervises hundreds of events occurring over these last few minutes. T minus 2 minutes 45 seconds and counting.

Jack King @JKLaunchControl
The members of the launch team here in the control center are monitoring a number of 'red line values'. These are tolerances we don't want to go above or below in temperatures and pressures. They are standing by to call out any deviations from our plans.

Jack King @JKLaunchControl
The vehicle is starting to pressurize as far as the propellant tanks are concerned and all is still GO at this time as we monitor our status board.

Jack King @JKLaunchControl
Two minutes 10 seconds and counting.

Jack King @JKLaunchControl
The target for the Apollo 11 astronauts, the Moon, at lift off will be at a distance of 218,096 miles away. We have just passed the two-minute mark in the countdown. T minus 1 minute 54 seconds and counting.

Jack King @JKLaunchControl
Our status board indicates that the oxidizer tanks in the second and third stages now have pressurized. We continue to build up pressure in all three stages at the last minute to prepare us for lift off.

Jack King @JKLaunchControl
T minus one minute 35 seconds on the Apollo 11 mission – the flight to land the first men on the Moon. All indications coming into the control center at this time indicate we are GO for launch.

Jack King @JKLaunchControl
Our status board indicates that all three stages are now completely pressurized. The 80-second mark has now been passed. We will go on full internal power at the 50-second mark in the countdown.

Jack King @JKLaunchControl
Guidance system goes on internal power at 17 seconds, leading up to the ignition sequence at 8.9 seconds. We are approaching the 60-second mark on the Apollo 11 mission.

Jack King @JKLaunchControl
Fifty-five seconds and counting. Neil Armstrong just reported back that, "It's been a real smooth countdown."

Jack King @JKLaunchControl
We have passed the 50-second mark. Power transfer is complete. We are on internal power with the launch vehicle at this time. Forty seconds away from lift off of Apollo 11.

Jack King @JKLaunchControl
We are still GO with Apollo 11. Astronauts report, "It feels good." Thirty seconds and counting.

Jack King @JKLaunchControl
T minus 25 seconds....

Jack King @JKLaunchControl
...20 seconds and counting.

Jack King @JKLaunchControl
T minus 15 seconds. Guidance is now internal.

Jack King @JKLaunchControl
12... 11... 10... 9... ignition sequence starts.

Jack King @JKLaunchControl
6... 5... 4 ...3... 2... 1... zero! All engines running...

Jack King @JKLaunchControl
Lift off! We have lift off!

Jack King @JKLaunchControl
Thirty-two minutes past the hour and we have lift off of Apollo 11!

Walter Cronkite @WCCBSNews
Oh, boy!...Oh, boy... Look at that!... it looks good!...Real good!

Neil Armstrong @CMDRApollo11
We have a roll program as expected.

Bruce McCandless @BMCAPCOM
We are confirming roll program from the ground.

Jack King @JKLaunchControl
Tower has been cleared and we have a roll program.

Neil Armstrong @CMDRApollo11
Roll is complete and the pitch is programmed.

Jack King @JKLaunchControl
Apollo 11 is looking good at 1 minute.

Jack King @JKLaunchControl
Altitude 2 miles. Downrange 1 mile. Altitude 3... 4 miles now. Velocity 2,195 feet per second. We are through the region of maximum dynamic pressure now.

Jack King @JKLaunchControl
Eight miles downrange, 12 miles high. Velocity 4,000 feet per second.

Clifford E. Charlesworth @CliffFlgtApollo11
Apollo 11 is GO for staging.

Bruce McCandless @BMCAPCOM
Apollo 11 is now GO for staging – first stage booster separation.

Bruce McCandless @BMCAPCOM
Downrange 35 miles, 30 miles high. Standing by for the inboard engine cut off.

Neil Armstrong @CMDRApollo11
Now initiating staging and ignition.

Clifford E. Charlesworth @CliffFlgtApollo11
Inboard engine cut off has been confirmed.

Walter Cronkite @WCCBSNews
Astronaut Wally Schirra is confirming my layman's observation that the trajectory looks real good right now.

Neil Armstrong @CMDRApollo11
Inboard engine cut-off occurred on schedule.

Bruce McCandless @BMCAPCOM
We confirm inboard engine cut-off at this time.

Bruce McCandless @BMCAPCOM
Thrust is good on all Apollo 11 engines. They're looking good at 3 minutes in.

Bruce McCandless @BMCAPCOM
Apollo 11 remains GO at 4 minutes.

Neil Armstrong @CMDRApollo11
Bruce is sure coming up loud and clear. Sounds like he's in his living room.

Bruce McCandless @BMCAPCOM
Voice on Apollo 11 is coming down clear too. Six minutes into the flight now.

Neil Armstrong @CMDRApollo11
We are starting the gimbal motors.

Walter Cronkite @WCCBSNews
Amazing channel that NASA has that we can still see the spacecraft even though it is 93 miles high, travelling at 8,000 miles an hour. It has to go up to 17,500 mph to get into Earth orbit.

Bruce McCandless @BMCAPCOM
Apollo 11 remains GO at 7 minutes.

Walter Cronkite @WCCBSNews
Looks like another perfect on-time Saturn V rocket launch. Something we've come to expect after the early days and delays of Mercury and Gemini, in that we now have these on-time Saturn launches.

Walter Cronkite @WCCBSNews
I wish we could get American railroads to run on the kind of schedule that Ron Brown and company get the Apollo launches to adhere to.

Bruce McCandless @BMCAPCOM
Apollo 11 is GO for next staging.

Neil Armstrong @CMDRApollo11
Staging and engine ignition completed.

Bruce McCandless @BMCAPCOM
Ignition is confirmed on our instruments. Thrust looks good. Apollo 11 remains a GO at 10 minutes on the clock.

Bruce McCandless @BMCAPCOM
Predicted cut-off is at 11 minutes 42 seconds. Apollo 11 remains GO at 11 minutes.

Neil Armstrong @CMDRApollo11
Shutdown at 11 minutes 42 seconds.

Bruce McCandless @BMCAPCOM
We confirm shutdown. Apollo 11 is now GO for orbit.

Neil Armstrong @CMDRApollo11
Our insertion to orbit checklist is now complete and we have no abnormalities.

Walter Cronkite @WCCBSNews
We should get confirmation of orbital insertion in about 15 seconds now.

Neil Armstrong @CMDRApollo11
We are now entering Earth orbit.

Bruce McCandless @BMCAPCOM
Radar from the Canary Island station is now showing Apollo 11 in a perfectly balanced orbit... beautiful!

Walter Cronkite @WCCBSNews
The orbit for the spacecraft has now been confirmed. So the first big jump in this trip to land a man on the Moon has been successfully completed.

Walter Cronkite @WCCBSNews
We now see Vice-President Agnew shaking hands with the dignitaries in the VVVIP viewing stand.

Walter Cronkite @WCCBSNews
When the spacecraft is over the Pacific ocean on its second orbit, they will fire off the S-IV third stage and boost their speed from 17,500 to 25,000 mph, which will put them on the way to the Moon.

Walter Cronkite @WCCBSNews
That Moon-trajectory speed is just enough to escape enough of the Earth's gravity to get to be captured by the Moon's gravity, to be brought around the far side of the Moon with enough inertial speed to come back to Earth.

Walter Cronkite @WCCBSNews
That speed and trajectory would not put them into Moon orbit or have them going so fast that they would bypass the Moon, not be caught by the Earth's gravity

and go on out to the Sun. Further adjustment burns will be needed later.

Bruce McCandless @BMCAPCOM
We continue reading Apollo 11 loud and clear. Both the booster and the spacecraft are looking good to us at this point.

Walter Cronkite @WCCBSNews
Apollo 11 is on the way now, having ridden that pillar of flame from the Saturn V rocket en-route to the Moon 250,000 miles away.

Walter Cronkite @WCCBSNews
The flight will take 3 days. The spacecraft will reach the Moon on Saturday. The landing will take place on Sunday and Neil Armstrong will set foot on the Moon on Monday.

Buzz Aldrin @LMPApollo11
Mike has the Hasselblad camera now and is doing some Earth photography. Some really stunning views out there.

Walter Cronkite @WCCBSNews
Apollo 11 is now over the Atlantic approaching the coast of Africa, then over the Indian Ocean, then over Australia and back for their first trip across the United States.

Walter Cronkite @WCCBSNews
On the second trip around, they will launch themselves out towards the Moon. We are being told that after this first trip around, we can expect a color TV transmission from the spacecraft.

Neil Armstrong @CMDRApollo11
Oh, man! Look at that view!

Walter Cronkite @WCCBSNews
Looking at my palms here following the launch, I see
they are extremely sweaty. Astronaut Wally Schirra
sitting next to me tells me that means I am now part
of the mission launch team.

Walter Cronkite @WCCBSNews
Wally had told me earlier that he has found, and
checked it out, that precisely three minutes before
launch, all astronauts' palms become sweaty. I
checked mine, so I at least qualify as an astronaut
according to the 'wet palm index'.

Walter Cronkite @WCCBSNews
I'm about to have a talk with Vice-President Spiro Agnew who is here today to represent President Nixon, and also in his current capacity as Head of the Space Council.

Spiro Agnew @SAgnewUSVeep
This one seemed to go easier than the others, but some things still scare the dickens out of me – like the lean out at the start after the rocket clears the tower. That IS scary.

Walter Cronkite @WCCBSNews
The slow climb is also pretty frightening. Even though you know it's going to be that way, you just can't believe that the vehicle is actually moving in those first few seconds.

Spiro Agnew @SAgnewUSVeep
It's like you are waiting for the thing to take off very quickly and it doesn't happen that way. But what a beautiful thing we have witnessed this morning!

Walter Cronkite @WCCBSNews
When it went up, there were tears in the eyes of many people. It's just something that happens to you – it's a real emotional release as you watch that thing go up. It must mean so much to the thousands of people who have put so much into this effort.

Spiro Agnew @SAgnewUSVeep
I just want to say that these people here are the greatest, most dedicated men I have ever run into, in or out of public life, military life... anywhere. They have a sense of purpose and a modesty that is overwhelming and yet so natural.

Walter Cronkite @WCCBSNews
I've just been handed a note informing me that the
Soviet news agency, TASS, has reported the launch of
Apollo 11. However, Russian TV did not broadcast the
launch live even though most of the rest of the world
did.

Walter Cronkite @WCCBSNews
I wonder if the Soviet news agency gave any details
about the purpose of their own Moon mission which
we believe is currently underway. If past Soviet space
missions are anything to go by — probably not.

Bruce McCandless @BMCAPCOM
We are seeing pitch and yaw on our instruments down
here in Mission Control, Houston. We are not seeing
roll yet.

Neil Armstrong @CMDRApollo11
Sounds like I need to put in a couple more rolls so
Houston can pick it up.

Bruce McCandless @BMCAPCOM
Okay. We are getting the roll impulses on our
instruments now and Apollo 11 is looking good.

Walter Cronkite @WCCBSNews
We are told that the astronauts' heartbeats during lift
off were far below those each recorded during their
first Gemini flights. They have each had one flight
before – a Gemini flight in each case.

Walter Cronkite @WCCBSNews
Armstrong had a heart rate of 110 at lift off. He had
146 on his Gemini flight. Collins is down to 99. He had
125 on his first flight. Aldrin came in lowest at only
88. What cool, unexcitable test pilots these men are!

Walter Cronkite @WCCBSNews
I know my heart rate leading up to lift off, had it been measured, would have been far higher than those of these three brave and remarkably calm astronauts. I certainly had incredibly sweaty palms.

Michael Collins @CMPApollo11
Getting a lot of 'squeel' on our headphones right now. Real hard to hear what Houston is trying to tell us.

Bruce McCandless @BMCAPCOM
We've handed the computer back to Apollo 11 now. Waiting to hear if they've extended the capture probe yet or not.

Bruce McCandless @BMCAPCOM
MILA apparently received about 1 minute of a usable TV signal from inside Apollo 11, so it looks like the system is working.

Buzz Aldrin @LMPApollo11
We are reading Houston at strength 4 right now. It's a little scratchy with the occasional annoying squeal.

Bruce McCandless @BMCAPCOM
We are reading Apollo 11 at strength 5, readability about 3. Should be quite adequate.

Neil Armstrong @CMDRApollo11
Still getting quite a bit of static on the comms. The worrying thing is it's likely to get worse the farther out we get. This mission depends on constant, reliable contact with our people in Houston.

Lyndon B. Johnson @LBJ
Watching the awesome sight of the lift off this morning, I was filled with great concern. I think all of

us will have great concern until this mission is concluded and our men are brought safely back to Earth as was President Kennedy's goal stated all those years ago when I was vice president.

Lyndon B. Johnson @LBJ
Another thought I had was that if we can do such a wonderful and complicated thing as a manned mission to the Moon, surely we must be able to do the work of bringing peace to the world.

Lyndon B. Johnson @LBJ
I do not believe that there is a single thing our country does, our government does, our people do, that has greater potential to bring peace to mankind than our space program.

Lyndon B. Johnson @LBJ
As I sat in that special section to watch the launch, with leaders and ambassadors from all the nations of the world, all taking such great pride in America's effort, all entertaining such great hope for the success of this mission, I felt an overwhelming sense of global unity.

Jules Bergman @JBABC News
Incredible to think that over 500,000 people have worked on this program in various capacities leading up to today's successful launch. What a wonderful combined effort it has been!

Jules Bergman (1929 – 1987)

Jules Bergman was a writer, broadcaster and journalist. He began covering developments in space exploration during the 1950s and went on to cover the entirety of the Mercury, Gemini, Apollo, Skylab and Apollo-Soyuz programs for ABC TV News network. He remained Science Editor for ABC News from 1961 until his death in 1987. He is most remembered for his coverage of the Apollo Moon missions.

He also covered the Space Shuttle program from its first flights through the 1986 Challenger disaster. In order to more fully understand the astronauts and their missions, Bergman often took part in the same training and simulations that the astronauts did.

Jules Bergman @JBABC News
Two hours 44 minutes after lift-off, the third stage rocket will ignite getting Apollo 11 up to escape velocity, 25,000 mph, overcoming the Earth's gravity and heading the spaceship out toward the Moon.

Bruce McCandless @BMCAPCOM
Apollo 11 is about to leave Earth orbit. Slightly less than 1 minute to ignition and everything is GO.

Michael Collins @CMPApollo11
We have ignition at 2 hours 44 minutes and 19 seconds. Engine is burning.

Bruce McCandless @BMCAPCOM
We confirm ignition on our instruments. Thrust looks good at 1 minute. Trajectory and guidance are also good.

Bruce McCandless @BMCAPCOM
Three and a half minutes into the burn and Apollo 11 looks good. Predicted cut-off is right on the nominal.

Neil Armstrong @CMDRApollo11
Houston confirms we remain GO at five minutes into the burn.

Bruce McCandless @BMCAPCOM
We read cut-off. Apollo 11 has now left Earth orbit and is heading toward the Moon.

Neil Armstrong @CMDRApollo11
That Saturn rocket sure gave us a magnificent ride. We have no complaints with any of the three stages. It was beautiful!

Walter Cronkite @WCCBSNews
While the American Apollo 11 mission has now left Earth orbit and set off on its journey to the Moon, we are learning more about the Soviet spaceship also on its way to the same destination.

Walter Cronkite @WCCBSNews
The head of Britain's Jodrell Bank radio telescope, Sir Bernard Lovell, is certain the Soviet spaceship is unmanned, but may be intended to gather Moon rocks and bring them back to Earth.

Bernard Lovell @BLJodrellBank
I am in the interesting position of listening to Apollo 11 in one ear and the Soviet spaceship, named Luna-15, in the other ear.

Walter Cronkite @WCCBSNews
There is no further detail on what the Russian spacecraft is supposed to do. Presumably, after it has completed its mission (whatever that is), we will learn what it did. That's the way the Russians do things.

Walter Cronkite @WCCBSNews
Meanwhile, Apollo 11 is now well on its way on its journey to the Moon, on an exact trajectory and velocity that was predicted by the boffins at NASA many months, even years, ago.

Rev. Ralph Albernathy @RevRalph
As I watched the launch to the Moon, I nearly forgot the fact that we have so many hungry people on this planet. Despite my deep reservations of this project, I was one of the proudest Americans as I stood on this spot at that time.

Spiro Agnew @SAgnewUSVeep
I am so excited by this! We are cleared already for missions Apollo 12 though Apollo 21 in the existing Apollo program which will continue with the exploration of the Moon.

Spiro Agnew @SAgnewUSVeep
I think we shouldn't be too timid to say, for example, that by the end of this century, we're going to put a man on Mars. The way science has developed in the last 50 years, I believe we will have the capability.

Bruce McCandless @BMCAPCOM
Apollo 11 should be maneuvering now to turn around and dock with lunar module Eagle prior to extraction. Unfortunately, we are out of comms right now.

Lunar module Eagle housed in the nose of the Saturn-IVB booster just prior to capture by the command module

Bruce McCandless @BMCAPCOM
I've been trying for over three minutes to contact Apollo 11. Still no success. Nothing at all coming down over comms.

Bruce McCandless @BMCAPCOM
Seven minutes and still no contact with Apollo 11.

Bruce McCandless @BMCAPCOM
Okay, we are now copying Apollo 11, but still very weak. I asked for a status report on the docking.

Neil Armstrong @CMDRApollo11
We are now docked with lunar module Eagle and have acquisition with the high-gain antenna at this time… I think.

Bruce McCandless @BMCAPCOM
Neil is coming in loud and clear right now, but Mike Collins is barely readable. However, we understand that they have successfully docked with Eagle.

Jules Bergman @JBABCNews
The Apollo 11 astronauts seem to have successfully separated from their burned-out booster, turned the spacecraft around and maneuvered back in to dock with Eagle – their lunar module.

Jules Bergman @JBABCNews
If the docking with the lunar module went exactly as planned, after checking out connections with the Eagle, the astronauts will have extracted Eagle from the burned-out booster.

Michael Collins @CMPApollo11
The docking with Eagle went pretty well, although I used more gas than I have ever done in the simulator.

Michael Collins @CMPApollo11
The turnaround maneuver was pretty tricky. I was pitching and drifting away from the Saturn-IVB more than I expected. I expected to be out about 66 feet, but it turned out to be 100 feet or so.

Michael Collins @CMPApollo11
So I used a bit more gas coming in to dock with Eagle. But except for using a little more gas, I'd say everything went nominally.

Bruce McCandless @BMCAPCOM
The Apollo 11 crew continue to work on the pressurization of lunar module Eagle now that it is attached to the command module. They are up to step 13 on the procedure at this point.

Buzz Aldrin @LMPApollo11
We have gone through most of the systems checks and lunar module Eagle appears to be in real fine shape right now.

Bruce McCandless @BMCAPCOM
We are about to do a non-propulsive vent from the booster at this time. Apollo 11 may see some sort of cloud coming out of it, but when they are ready we have their evasive maneuver procedure prepared for upload.

Neil Armstrong @CMDRApollo11
We see the cloud coming out from the separated booster now. It's a haze and going by toward our

minus-X direction. Several small particles are moving along with it with quite a high velocity.

Neil Armstrong @CMDRApollo11
Houston and the people on Earth might be interested to know that I can now observe the entire continent of North America, Alaska, over the Pole and down to the Yukatan Peninsula, Cuba, northern South America and then I run out of window.

Bruce McCandless @BMCAPCOM
Apollo 11 has confirmed that all 12 latches between the two vehicles (Columbia and Eagle) are now locked.

Bruce McCandless @BMCAPCOM
I was halfway through reading up the evasion procedure to Apollo 11 when the comms cut off, probably due to the signal handover to Madrid. I may have to start again.

Bruce McCandless @BMCAPCOM
I guess the view up there must be pretty good. Michael Collins and Buzz are waxing pretty rapturous about it.

Buzz Aldrin @LMPApollo11
I can still see the snow on the mountains out in California, and it looks like LA doesn't have much of a smog problem today.

Earth view from Apollo 11

Bruce McCandless @BMCAPCOM
We are continuing with the non-propulsion vent from the S-IVB. We're also dumping a small amount of fuel.

Buzz Aldrin @LMPApollo11
We have the detached S-IV booster in sight now. It appears to be a couple of miles away and we can see the venting coming from two radially opposite directions.

Bruce McCandless @BMCAPCOM
We have a recommended configuration for their CRYO switches to even up the load between oxygen tanks 1 and 2. I'll read it up shortly.

Buzz Aldrin @LMPApollo11
If the guys in Houston are wondering why we've been late in answering them recently, it's because we're munching sandwiches.

Michael Collins @CMPApollo11
Bruce at Mission Control just said he wished he could have a sandwich right now. I told him, in no uncertain terms, not to leave his console. He assured me he wouldn't.

Neil Armstrong @CMDRApollo11
I think today is California's 200th. birthday so we wish all Californians a happy birthday from space. I believe it is also Dr. Mueller's birthday, though I don't think he's quite that old.

Bruce McCandless @BMCAPCOM
I will pass on Apollo 11's birthday greetings to Dr. Mueller when he gets back from the Cape. Meanwhile, we'd like Neil to do a wastewater dump to 5 percent remaining.

Bruce McCandless @BMCAPCOM
We're going to hand over to Hawaii in the next few seconds and expect a momentary comms dropout. Hopefully, not too long. About to hand over to Charlie Duke and his White Team.

Charlie Duke @CDCAPCOM
I have advised Apollo 11 that their friendly White Team has now come on for its first shift and that if we can be of service, they should not hesitate to call.

Charlie Duke @CDCAPCOM
First order of business is to have Apollo 11 turn on the fan in oxygen tank number 2.

Buzz Aldrin @LMPApollo11
I've got a CRYO pressure warning light and a MASTER ALARM!

Charlie Duke @CDCAPCOM
We were kind of expecting that alarm and hoping to avoid it. That's why we had them turn the oxygen tank fan on.

Buzz Aldrin @LMPApollo11
No problem. The CRYO indicators are reset now. But I would hope we can avoid getting these MASTER ALARMS if at all possible – they're pretty unnerving.

Charlie Duke @CDCAPCOM
We will be charging up battery B from now until the sleep period when we will discontinue charging. The scheduled battery A charge has been deleted.

Michael Collins @CMPApollo11
I'm trying to get good stars in the sextant right now. Star 40 has just disappeared. Houston asked me to move on to star 44, but that one has a reddish glow filling the sextant and I can't see the star clearly.

Charlie Duke @CDCAPCOM
We're recommending Mike move on to star 45. The 3 gimbal angles we gave him for star 44 should be valid for star 45 as well.

Michael Collins @CMPApollo11
I think there's something wrong with these attitudes. I'm inclined not to believe the program from what I'm seeing out of the window. I'm going to trim up the attitudes and give it another try.

Michael Collins @CMPApollo11
Okay. I have star 45 in the clear now, so I might as well do a bunch of marks on this one to get a good horizon count.

Charlie Duke @CDCAPCOM
We'd like 6 marks on star 45 and have Mike move back to star 2, or maybe other stars. We'll have further word on that later – the procedures people are working hard on this right now.

Michael Collins @CMPApollo11
The difficulty is in getting two stars that are not occulted by the lunar module and are also not in a man-made star field up here created by our wastewater dumps.

Charlie Duke @CDCAPCOM
Handing the computer back to Apollo 11.

Charlie Duke @CDCAPCOM
Apollo 11's attitude at present is really bad for our comms. In fact, we've lost all data and voice is unreadable right now. Hope Mike can figure out a good attitude adjustment. It's pretty much trial and error at this point.

Michael Collins @CMPApollo11
Okay. We're getting Charlie Duke and Mission Control loud and clear now. We pitched down to get a better comms attitude and it seems to have worked.

Michael Collins @CMPApollo11
I have verified the third star with Antares and AUTO optics are pointing at it pretty closely.

10 hours 4 minutes mission time

Walter Cronkite @WCCBSNews
Apollo 11 is now well on its way to the Moon with no major concerns at this time. In fact, the surprising

thing about this first day of the Apollo mission is that the Soviet Moon mission made more news.

Walter Cronkite @WCCBSNews
The apparently-unmanned Luna-15 spacecraft appears to have gone into a close in orbit around the Moon.

Walter Cronkite @WCCBSNews
Moscow is officially saying little, but there is much guesswork that the spacecraft will attempt a soft landing on the Moon and perhaps try to return some lunar surface material to Earth before Apollo 11 does.

Neil Armstrong @CMDRApollo11
We are sending TV pictures of Earth down, zooming in right now. Houston will let us know if they are receiving the pictures at the Goldstone station.

Neil Armstrong @CMDRApollo11
Our TV pictures will be recorded down at Goldstone station and then patched over to Houston.

Charlie Duke @CDCAPCOM
Goldstone is telling us that they are receiving the TV signal from Apollo 11 and that the quality looks great.

Charlie Duke @CDCAPCOM
Comments from Goldstone indicate there are no white spots in the pictures such as those we had on Apollo 10. The f-22 camera setting looks good apparently.

Neil Armstrong @CMDRApollo11
Houston has asked us to continue with the TV for another ten minutes or so. We can film anything we think interesting: interior, exterior, pan in and out and add some narrative. Anything we like.

Buzz Aldrin @LMPApollo11
Nice to have been granted some artistic license with
our filmmaking career.

Buzz Aldrin @LMPApollo11
There is something moving alongside of us and we
don't know what it is. It can't be the Saturn IV
booster, so it's quite a mystery.

Buzz Aldrin @LMPApollo11
Maybe the Russians have sent us a chaperone for our
journey to the Moon. Hopefully, Houston can figure it
out.

Charlie Duke @CDCAPCOM
We need Apollo 11 to turn their CRYO heaters to AUTO
at this time and turn off all four CRYO fans. That is
going to be their sleep configuration. We'll also be
terminating the battery charge in about 30 minutes.

Charlie Duke @CDCAPCOM
We have been noting some funnies on the oxygen flow
indicator. Also some strange indications when they
closed the waste stowage vent valve. We're going to
continue to look at this through the night and get back
to them in the morning.

Michael Collins @CMPApollo11
Time for some food before bedtime. Charlie Duke is
recommending the peanut and jelly.

22 hours 50 minutes mission time

Dan Rather @DRCBSNews
The Apollo 11 astronauts are carrying to the Moon the
medals and insignias of their colleagues who died in
the fire on the launch pad of Apollo 1. And, it has now

been revealed by the White House, something else as well.

Richard M. Nixon @RMNUSPresident
When Apollo 8 astronaut Frank Borman was in the Soviet Union recently, he was presented two medals from the wives of the Russian cosmonauts who lost their lives in the Soviet space program – their husbands' posthumous medals.

Richard M. Nixon @RMNUSPresident
At the request of those wives, Neil Armstrong and Buzz Aldrin will leave their husbands' medals on the surface of the Moon.

Richard M. Nixon @RMNUSPresident
Honoring in this way those who gave their lives in the space program, both American and Soviet, illustrates the true spirit of the American military – we maintain strength, but we maintain it because we want peace.

Bruce McCandless @BMCAPCOM
The Apollo 13 astronauts are up and about now. We have just run through a bunch of stuff with them. Mainly regarding battery charging issues. Time to read up the morning news to our guys in space.

Bruce McCandless @BMCAPCOM
Britain's big Jodrell Bank radio telescope has stopped receiving signals from the Soviet Union's unmanned Moon probe. It seems the Luna-15 spaceship may have gone beyond the Moon and not landed. They are not sure at this point.

Bruce McCandless @BMCAPCOM
Vice President Spiro Agnew has called for putting a man on Mars by the year 2000. Agnew was apparently speaking for himself and not the Nixon administration.

Bruce McCandless @BMCAPCOM
Immigration officials in Nuevo Laredo say that hippies will be refused tourist cards to enter Mexico unless they take a bath and get haircuts. This following complaints by Mexico City and other authorities about the hippies.

Bruce McCandless @BMCAPCOM
President Nixon has granted a holiday to federal employees Monday so they can observe a 'National Day of Participation' in the Moon landing mission.

Bruce McCandless @BMCAPCOM
The headline in France's Le Figaro newspaper stated today that "The Greatest Adventure In The History of Humanity Has Started!" It devoted several pages to the mission of Apollo 11, as did most European newspapers.

1 day 0 hours 11 minutes mission time

Neil Armstrong @CMDRApollo11
Getting ready to do an oxygen fuel cell purge. Houston wants me to do them one at a time (not to triple up), but to do them in no particular order. The fuel cell purge has triggered the MASTER ALARM three times now.

Neil Armstrong @CMDRApollo11
We now have a fourth MASTER ALARM!

Bruce McCandless @BMCAPCOM
Down here, we read that the oxygen flow on fuel cell 3 was flowing a little higher than the other two during the purge. However, the flow rate remains at an acceptable rate.

Michael Collins @CMPApollo11
Fuel cell 3 is certainly flowing more than the other two. It is also actually putting out more current than the other two.

Bruce McCandless @BMCAPCOM
We are continuing to monitor the flow rate from the fuel cells. Now handing back the computer to Apollo 11.

Bruce McCandless @BMCAPCOM
Over the past 2 hours, we have seen a slight continuing increase in their CO_2 levels. We need to know if they have changed the CO_2 scrubbing canister yet this morning.

Michael Collins @CMPApollo11
We haven't changed any CO_2 scrubbing canisters yet. I'll get onto it shortly.

Eric Sevaroid @ESCBSNews
Soon after this mission is over, politics will pick up again almost, but not quite, where it left off BM – Before Moon. The fundamental argument here in Washington is how we use our money and resources in the AM – After Moon.

Eric Sevaroid @ESCBSNews
Space may be infinite, but the federal budget is not. There is a powerful push here to reduce our prodigious

military expenditure, and a fairly strong push to reduce our expenditures on space.

Eric Sevaroid @ESCBSNews
The irony of the situation is that a successful Apollo 11 mission is more likely to herald a stretch out of the space program than failure. Failure, with the Russians breathing down our necks, would mean redoubled effort.

Eric Sevareid (1912 – 1992)

Eric Sevareid was a prominent CBS news reporter and war correspondent from 1939 to 1977. He was the first to report the fall of Paris when it was captured by the Germans in 1939. In the 1960s, along with Walter Cronkite, he gave extensive commentary on the assassination of President John F. Kennedy, the Apollo program and the Vietnam War. Unlike many journalists, Sevareid was considered to be a reporter with 'attitude' and openly admitted to his own political biases.

Eric Sevaroid @ESCBSNews
Yesterday, the congressmen watching the launch seemed united around the common goal. Unlike most political issues and projects, the Apollo 11 mission has a beginning, a middle and an end.

Eric Sevaroid @ESCBSNews
At the moment of the launch all political and financial considerations of those present were vaporized and vanished. But they will reappear soon, for politics, as Doctor Einstein once said, is more difficult than physics.

Michael Collins @CMPApollo11
The Earth is still pretty bright, and the black sky, instead of being black has a sort of rosy glow to it. The star I'm looking for is probably lost inside that glow.

Michael Collins @CMPApollo11
I maneuvered considerably above the horizon to make sure the star is not lost in the brightness below the horizon. However, even when I get above the horizon so the star should be seen against the black background, it's still not visible.

Michael Collins @CMPApollo11
It really is a fantastic sight through the sextant. A minute ago, I could see all of North Africa absolutely clearly. All of Spain, Portugal, southern France and all of Italy. Absolutely clear. Just a beautiful sight!

Michael Collins @CMPApollo11
But still no orientation and navigation star.

Bruce McCandless @BMCAPCOM
Our ground computers indicate that the angle Mike has should be pointing at the star. However, it looks as if the angle is also pointing into the structure of the lunar module. While he is getting the Earth's horizon, the star is being obscured by Eagle.

Bruce McCandless @BMCAPCOM
We are recommending an AUTO maneuver to the attitudes pen-and-inked into the flight plan. Roll: 1772. Pitch: 2982. Yaw: 330.0

Michael Collins @CMPApollo11
Okay. Our maneuver is complete. We are now pointed along the vector to the center of the Earth instead of being parallel to the right. After the slight change in attitude, I now have a star.

Bruce McCandless @BMCAPCOM
Apollo 11 is now a little more than an hour to their mid-course correction. They need to press on with their wastewater dump and get ready for the burn. I'm reading up the technical coordinates and timings now.

Bruce McCandless @BMCAPCOM
We're having more problems with the comms right now. I had to repeat the roll, pitch and yaw coordinates several times.

Neil Armstrong @CMDRApollo11
I am about to conduct our mid-course correction engine burn.

Neil Armstrong @CMDRApollo11
I think we have everything in order for the burn.

Neil Armstrong @CMDRApollo11
Initiating the burn in 4... 3... 2... 1...BURN!

Bruce McCandless @BMCAPCOM
We are copying Apollo 11's mid-course correction burn on our instruments.

Neil Armstrong @CMDRApollo11
Burn completed. Shutdown.

Bruce McCandless @BMCAPCOM
No problem with the burn. The spaceship is now starting PTC maneuvers. From a propellant-balancing viewpoint, we recommend they use quads Alpha and Bravo.

Bruce McCandless @BMCAPCOM
For CRYO-balancing purposes, we'd like them to turn the heater and oxygen tank number 1 off at this time.

1 day 3 hours 17 minutes mission time

Buzz Aldrin @LMPApollo11
I'm looking through the monocular now and, to coin an expression, the view is just "out of this world". I can see all the islands in the Mediterranean and some cumulus clouds over Greece.

Buzz Aldrin @LMPApollo11
The Sun is setting on the eastern Mediterranean now. The British Isles are definitely greener in color than the brownish-green of the Iberian peninsula and its islands.

Buzz Aldrin @LMPApollo11
The islands in the Caribbean are starting to come up now. This monocular is a pretty good instrument, but it could do with another order of magnification and maybe some kind of bracket to hold it steady.

Buzz Aldrin @LMPApollo11
I've been having a ball floating around in here, back and forth up to one place and back to another. It sure is a hell of a lot bigger than the Gemini vehicle Jim Lovell and I were in.

Buzz Aldrin @LMPApollo11
I've been very busy so far, but I'm looking forward to taking the afternoon off. I've been cooking, sweeping and almost sewing. You know, the usual little housekeeping things.

1 day 3 hours 53 minutes mission time

Michael Collins @CMPApollo11
I'm looking back at the world through the monocular again. It's really something. I wish I could describe it properly. South America is coming round into view and I can see all the way from Seattle, Washington to the southern tip of Tierra del Fuego.

Buzz Aldrin @LMPApollo11
We're just tucking into some salmon salad. My compliments to the chef. It's quite outstanding.

Bruce McCandless @BMCAPCOM
Charlie Duke is about to take over my CAPCOM chair. Meanwhile, Mike and Buzz sound like they've got a table at one of those expensive, sky-high rotating restaurants.

Charlie Duke @CDCAPCOM
The infamous White Team is now back on duty. We're all bright-eyed and bushy-tailed, ready to take on whatever may come.

Michael Collins @CMPApollo11
I asked Charlie Duke to have the medics look at my biomed telemetry. I'm trying some running in place and wondering out of curiosity if it's bumping up my heart rate.

Charlie Duke @CDCAPCOM
Medics have sprung into action and report that Mike Collins' heart does actually beat. Currently at a rate of 96 beats per minute.

Charlie Duke @CDCAPCOM
About to read up a whole heap of coordinates, electrical, environmental and attitude adjustment settings to Apollo 11. Nothing of general interest to note down here, but of vital interest to the crew in space.

Charlie Duke @CDCAPCOM
Apollo 11 is now 125,200 miles out, travelling at 4,486 feet per second.

Michael Collins @CMPApollo11
I'm curious to know what is going on with the Soviet spaceship. Wondering if it is some kind of competitor to our mission.

Charlie Duke @CDCAPCOM
Sir Bernard Lovell at Jodrell Bank in England tells us the Soviets' Luna-15 spacecraft has now been located in a lunar orbit of around 62 nautical miles and appears to be functioning normally.

Charlie Duke @CDCAPCOM
Not only are federal employees being given the day off on Monday by the president. A large number of private companies are allowing their employees to stay home and follow the activities on the Moon's surface.

Michael Collins @CMPApollo11
Nice that Neil and Buzz will have a large live audience for their moonwalks. I'll just be going round and round the Moon in my lonely spaceship hoping the guys make it back to orbit safely.

Charlie Duke @CDCAPCOM
We're getting ready to monitor some more TV the crew will be sending down from Apollo 11.

Michael Collins @CMPApollo11
The three of us are pretty comfortable and we do have a happy home up here in zero gravity. There's actually plenty of room and we're all learning to find our own favorite little corner to settle down in, put our knees up and try to wedge ourselves in somewhere.

Charlie Duke @CDCAPCOM
We're really impressed with the TV pictures the crew is sending down right now. The clarity and detail are excellent.

Michael Collins @CMPApollo11
I'm filming Neil standing on his head again. He's trying to make me nervous. Now he's disappearing up the tunnel as if entering the lunar module, only backwards.

Michael Collins @CMPApollo11
Just boiled up some water, squeezed a tube of stuff into it and mushed it up, and there you go... beautiful chicken stew. The food so far has been very good. We couldn't be happier with it.

Philip Gibson @philiplaos
Those NASA astronauts really are made of special stuff. Unlike most of us, they never complain about minor stuff like the food and accommodation, and keep a calm sense of humor at all times. Really admirable.

Philip Gibson @philiplaos
I'm wondering if NASA screens potential astronauts for cheerful, uncomplaining character traits like that and weed out the fussy complainers from the program. I'll bet they do.

Charlie Duke @CDCAPCOM
We noticed pressure levels on the CRYOs dropped a moment ago. We need to know if the crew are remembering to stir the CRYOs regularly.

Charlie Duke @CDCAPCOM
We're now handing over comms from Goldstone to Honeysuckle stations and expect a brief gap while the signal is acquired and established.

Buzz Aldrin @LMPApollo11
Houston has confirmed that they are reading us fine through Honeysuckle.

Buzz Aldrin @LMPApollo11
I'm about to copy some numbers down to Houston. Many pages of numbers. No point in noting them

down here though – they only mean anything to the specialized technical guys in Mission Control.

Buzz Aldrin @LMPApollo11
I think Houston have all the numbers they need to work on now. While they get to work on those, we're going to turn in for the night.

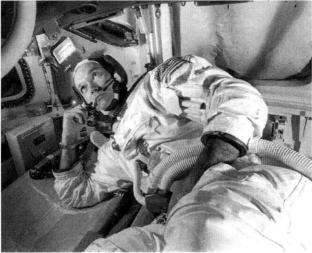

Mike Collins inside Columbia

Michael Collins @CMPApollo11
Another morning on Apollo 11 after an uneventful night's sleep. Bruce and his Green Team have taken over at Mission Control and they tell us that Ron Evans and his Black Team jokingly complained that they didn't get a chance to make any transmissions during the night.

Bruce McCandless @BMCAPCOM
Ron Evans is getting a reputation as 'the silent CAPCOM'. That won't last long. He and his team will be plenty busy tomorrow.

Bruce McCandless @BMCAPCOM
We need a wastewater dump at the crew's convenience. We're deleting midcourse correction number 3 and all the details associated with it. If we decide to burn midcourse correction number 4, it will be at 2.0 feet per second.

Bruce McCandless @BMCAPCOM
Buzz is reading down their consumables update now. Everything looks broadly in order although we are still getting a lot of noise and dropout on the comms signal.

Michael Collins @CMPApollo11
We're getting a CRYO pressure warning light in the middle of stirring up the CRYO tanks.

Bruce McCandless @BMCAPCOM
We're looking into the situation in the CRYO tanks. Meanwhile, the noise on the comms seems to have quieted down. I guess they've rotated another antenna into view.

Michael Collins @CMPApollo11
I'm not able to differentiate stars from the thousands of sparkling wastewater droplets after the wastewater we dumped into space several hours ago.

Bruce McCandless @BMCAPCOM
We had believed that interference from their wastewater dump would dissipate after about one hour to the point where they would be able to take star sightings for alignment/navigation. We may have been wrong on that one.

Michael Collins @CMPApollo11
The telescope is pretty much useless right now. However, we found we are able to use the sextant to differentiate between the water droplets and stars by observing the difference in their motions.

Buzz Aldrin @LMPApollo11
It looks like our oxygen flow has gotten a good bit worse. I just looked at the transducer at the last water accumulator cycling and it just barely registered.

Bruce McCandless @BMCAPCOM
We think the oxygen flow transducer is malfunctioning due to the stroking the crew have been doing. It's probably going to keep on getting worse.

Bruce McCandless @BMCAPCOM
However, it's an instrumentation problem only. We believe actual oxygen flow remains nominal. Nothing to worry about. I'm about to read up the morning news to the Apollo 11 crew.

Bruce McCandless @BMCAPCOM
Interest in the Apollo 11 mission remains high all around the world. However, a competing interest in the Houston area is the imminent easing of lawn-watering restrictions if the rains continue.

Bruce McCandless @BMCAPCOM
The Norwegian explorer, Thor Hayerdahl has said that the crew of his papyrus boat Ra will sail the boat into Bridgetown, Barbados, despite heavy damage from the recent storm.

Bruce McCandless @BMCAPCOM
In sports, the Houston Oilers are showing plenty of enthusiasm in their pre-season workouts, and coach

Wally Lemm says he's impressed with the fine group of rookies.

Bruce McCandless @BMCAPCOM
In Corby, England, an Irishman, John Coyle, has won the world's porridge-eating competition by consuming 32 bowls of instant oatmeal in a 10-minute time limit from a field of 35 competitors.

Michael Collins @CMPApollo11
I'd like to enter Aldrin in the oatmeal-eating competition next time - he's certainly doing his share up here. He's on his 19th. bowl right now.

Charlie Duke @CDCAPCOM
We're going to hand over the signal to Goldstone in about 2 minutes and expect a momentary dropout of comms.

Michael Collins @CMPApollo11
We have a MASTER ALARM going off right in the cabin right now. Looks like it's something to do with the oxygen flow rate.

Michael Collins @CMPApollo11
The photoelectric cell amplifier for the MASTER ALARM is a good device. Works well and is very loud. We can't fail to hear the alarms now. Would be more relaxing if we didn't keep getting them though.

Charlie Duke @CDCAPCOM
We are looking at valve positions on the oxygen flow systems and trying to figure out configurations that will reduce the number of MASTER ALARMS going off.

Neil Armstrong @CMDRApollo11
Looks like we'll be able to enter lunar module Eagle earlier than expected. We have permission from Houston to do so and so are going ahead.

Charlie Duke @CDCAPCOM
We're really amazed at the quality of the TV pictures up in the tunnel between the command module and lunar module Eagle. It's really superb!

Michael Collins @CMPApollo11
Buzz just opened the hatch to the lunar module and the light inside came on immediately. Just like the refrigerator back home. Neil is going through the tunnel now.

Charlie Duke @CDCAPCOM
We're watching Buzz Aldrin and Neil Armstrong waving at us from inside lunar module Eagle. Everything looks shipshape in there. Nothing is floating around and the TV pictures are excellent.

Neil Armstrong @CMDRApollo11
The lighting in the lunar module is very nice now, just like daylight. A good bit lighter than the tunnel was earlier.

Buzz Aldrin @LMPApollo11
The lunar module is surprisingly free of any debris floating around. We thought some stuff might have been shaken loose during lift off and the course correction burns, but apparently not. It's very clean in here.

Buzz Aldrin @LMPApollo11
We've got a beautiful view of the command module out of Eagle's rear left window. I can see the hatch

and all the EVA handrails. First time we've seen the silvery outside of the command module.

Buzz Aldrin @LMPApollo11
We don't have any circulation in lunar module Eagle, so it might start to get a little warm.

Walter Cronkite @WCCBSNews
Some wonderful TV shots we're seeing beamed down from Apollo 11 right now. A little fuzzy, but really quite remarkable considering they are now 203,000 miles out from the Earth.

Walter Cronkite @WCCBSNews
The spacecraft now just 43,000 miles from the Moon. We are seeing the windows on the lunar module which are two triangles, as well as the overhead window through which the astronauts are able to look and take their bearings.

The lunar module triangular windows

Charlie Duke @CDCAPCOM
Mike Collins just suggested putting a couple of hoses from the command module into the lunar module to get a little circulation going. Sounds like a good idea.

Buzz Aldrin @LMPApollo11
There is very little debris floating around in either the command module or the lunar module. We found very few loose nuts, bolts, screws, lint or other material. Both vehicles have made it this far very clean.

Charlie Duke @CDCAPCOM
Buzz is showing us pictures of Mike Collins in the command module filmed out of a lunar module window. We are able to make out his two staring eyes even through the several layers of glass.

Charlie Duke @CDCAPCOM
We see they have raised the cover on the ABORT panel inside the lunar module. We do not recommend that! Seriously! Buzz says he will tape it over as an added precaution and we definitely concur with that.

Neil Armstrong @CMDRApollo11
Houston just told me at this attitude I look like I'm about 12 feet long. It seems like I always find myself upside-down no matter what I'm doing around here.

Neil Armstrong @CMDRApollo11
The hoses from the command and service module are moving the air around pretty good now. I'd say the temperature is around 73 to 75 and the comfort level is about the same as in the command module.

The combined lunar module, command module and service module

Neil Armstrong @CMDRApollo11
It was a little warmer or stuffier when we first got in but it seems to be improving now. However, there are now quite a few dust particles floating around and we're choking on them every so often.

Charlie Duke @CDCAPCOM
The Apollo 11 TV show is now going out to U.S. viewers. We're about to get the satellite link up and running and it will then be broadcast to the rest of the world.

Buzz Aldrin @LMPApollo11
I'm checking out the window bracket where I'll be putting the camera for the EVA pictures when Neil climbs down the ladder and steps onto the surface of the Moon. Really want to get that sequence lined up right - the whole world may be watching.

Buzz Aldrin @LMPApollo11
The new knobs make it really easy to twist the bracket and get it cinched down real tight. The alignment looks good, but anyway there's nowhere else we could fix it to see much more out of the window without hand-holding the camera for the entire time.

Charlie Duke @CDCAPCOM
This broadcast, live from Apollo 11, has a pretty big TV audience. It's going out live in the U.S. It's going live to Japan, Western Europe and much of South America, and we sure do appreciate the great show.

Neil Armstrong @CMDRApollo11
Mike Collins is still sitting all by himself in the command module. We are willing to allow him into the lunar module for a brief look around, but he hasn't come up with the price of the ticket yet.

Charlie Duke @CDCAPCOM
If they do allow Mike into the Eagle, they should advise him to keep his hands off the switches. Neil has already asked him to keep his hands off the commander's switches in the command module while he is in the Eagle.

Michael Collins @CMPApollo11
This is why I've been eating so much today. They won't let me touch anything anymore.

Buzz Aldrin @LMPApollo11
Sending back some shots of the rapidly receding home planet now.

Charlie Duke @CDCAPCOM
If that's not the Earth, we're in trouble.

Neil Armstrong @CMDRApollo11
That IS the Earth, and we have had a very good view
of it today. There are a few more cloud bands than
when we beamed it down to Houston yesterday, but
it's a beautiful sight!

Buzz Aldrin @LMPApollo11
The folks on Earth might be interested to know that
we have cards where we log all the procedures and a
timeline book. Since we are in zero gravity, we put
Velcro patches on the back of every item and stick
them onto the table in front of the data display to stop
them floating around.

Buzz Aldrin @LMPApollo11
This must be the most unusual position a cameraman's ever had, hanging by his toes from a tunnel and filming upside-down.

Charlie Duke @CDCAPCOM
Buzz has a pretty big audience right now. It's live in the U.S. It's still going live to Japan, Western Europe and much of South America. Everybody reports very good color and that they appreciate the great show.

Charlie Duke @CDCAPCOM
Apollo 11 is now 177,000 miles out from Earth and the crew have completed the latest TV broadcast. Our thanks to Apollo 11 for one of the greatest TV shows we have ever seen. That was really appreciated down here.

Neil Armstrong @CMDRApollo11
We've still got a little work to do here in the Eagle before getting back to the command module. We want to make sure we have everything stowed away and try to get a little ahead of tomorrow's timeline.

Charlie Duke @CDCAPCOM
We need Apollo 11 to do a wastewater dump at about this time. All the way down to zero.

Neil Armstrong @CMDRApollo11
I just noticed that the EVA (extra-vehicular activity) light on the lunar module is on and is charred brown. It looks as though it took quite a beating during launch.

Charlie Duke @CDCAPCOM
We have some guys looking at what, if anything, we can do about the EVA light on the lunar module.

Charlie Duke @CDCAPCOM
Neil and Buzz will continue their familiarization with the lunar module conditions until about 58 hours and then get back into the command and service module with Mike Collins and close the hatch.

Charlie Duke @CDCAPCOM
We confirm that the latest wastewater dump has been completed. We need the crew to stir up the CRYO tanks at this time.

Neil Armstrong @CMDRApollo11
We have completed our inspection of lunar module Eagle and are now pulling the probe and drogue back in and closing up the hatches.

Charlie Duke @CDCAPCOM
Now all the crew are back in the command module we'll read up a bunch of technical procedures for them to copy. Mainly switch positions for the high gain, GO/NO-GO cards, and radiator leak check list settings.

Michael Collins @CMPApollo11
We're playing some horn music up here. After Houston asked me about it, I told them we're celebrating a special day here - today is the third anniversary of Gemini 10.

Charlie Duke @CDCAPCOM
We are concerned that the intermediate-scale and large-scale maps of the lunar landing sites seem not to be stored in Eagle where the crew expect them to be.

Charlie Duke @CDCAPCOM
We need to be sure Neil and Buzz have easy and rapid access to those maps when they are guiding Eagle down to the lunar surface. They only have a few seconds during the latter stages of the descent to get it right.

Charlie Duke @CDCAPCOM
We see Apollo 11 as drifting off course with a funny pattern that we haven't seen previously on a flight. We're trying to figure it out and will get back to the crew shortly.

Charlie Duke @CDCAPCOM
We have no assurance that we're going to get through this PTC procedure with this funny configuration before the crew's sleep period, so we intend to terminate the procedure for the moment.

Neil Armstrong @CMDRApollo11
I asked Houston where our discarded Saturn IV-B booster now is in relation to us. They said it's 6,000 miles away and, like us, still heading for an encounter with the lunar surface.

Charlie Duke @CDCAPCOM
Our White Team is now signing off and handing over to the evening shift. So it's goodnight from us.

2 days, 21 hours 10 minutes mission time

Walter Cronkite @WCCBSNews
It has been revealed today that NASA astronaut Frank Borman, who recently visited the Soviet Union, twice telephoned a top Russian scientist yesterday.

Walter Cronkite @WCCBSNews
Borman asked the Russian scientist for some precise details about the orbit of the Soviet Luna-15 spacecraft now apparently circling the Moon.

Walter Cronkite @WCCBSNews
The Russian scientist said the Luna-15 mission did not pose a threat to the Apollo 11 astronauts, but did not say what the purpose of the Russian mission is. We are still in the dark about that.

Ronald Evans @RECAPCOM
Just wished the sleepy crew of Apollo 11 a very good morning after an uneventful night's work monitoring the spacecraft from here at Mission Control, Houston.

Buzz Aldrin @LMPApollo11
Mid-course correction 4 has been deleted by Houston and we have been told we can turn over and get some more sleep until 71 hours if we like. Sounds good to me.

Buzz Aldrin @LMPApollo11
Neil and Mike slept 7.5 hours last night. 6.5 hours for me.

David Brinkley @DBNBCNews
Apollo 11 is now three-quarters of the way to the Moon, and we are assured that when they get there Luna-15, the unmanned Russian spacecraft will not get in their way.

David Brinkley @DBCABCNews
It is still not known if the Soviets intend to land Luna-15 on the Moon, scoop up some rocks, and return to Earth before Apollo 11 bring back their rock and soil samples.

Jules Bergman @JBABCNews
The next critical hurdle for Apollo 11 comes tomorrow afternoon when they do that big lunar orbit insertion burn – a big burn behind the Moon that will lower their orbit and drop the spacecraft into a 60 by 107 mile orbit.

Buzz Aldrin @LMPApollo11
Up again at 71 hours after nearly 2 hours more sleep than planned. About to do an oxygen fuel cell purge as requested by Houston. Also, another flight plan update is upcoming.

Ronald Evans @RECAPCOM
At 71-72 hours, we want the crew to have an eat period after the fuel cell purge. Then, a CO_2 filter change number 6 and secondary radiator flow check. Then, copy down some minor drift attitude adjustment coordinates and timings as well as an update to the latest preferred landing site.

Buzz Aldrin @LMPApollo11
Getting a real good view of the smaller topographical features on the Moon's surface now that we are so near. I can see the impact crater Tycho clearly illuminated by Earthshine.

Bruce McCandless @BMCAPCOM
We're asking Buzz to take some photos of various features on the Moon's surface at his discretion. He should use the electric Hasselblad camera with the 80 millimeter lens with an f stop of 2.8.

Bruce McCandless @BMCAPCOM
We're asking for exposures of an eighth of a second to half a second. If Buzz can steady the camera against

something to get longer exposures, 2, 4 and 8 second exposures, that would be great.

Neil Armstrong @CMDRApollo11
We're seeing a real change now. We're able to see stars and recognize constellations for the first time on this trip. The sky is full of stars. All the way here, we have only been able to see stars occasionally through the monocular, but not recognize any constellations.

Neil Armstrong @CMDRApollo11
We have completed the secondary radiator flow check. It is complete and satisfactory.

Bruce McCandless @BMCAPCOM
We're having difficulties getting commands uplinked into the spacecraft. They need to cycle their UP TELEMETRY, switch to COMMAND RESET to OFF and then back to NORMAL.

Bruce McCandless @BMCAPCOM
Telemetry and voice comms are now good again. Time to read up the morning news from Earth to the crew of Apollo 11, hot from the wires of the MSC Public Affairs office, specially prepared for the crew of Apollo 11.

Bruce McCandless @BMCAPCOM
Impossible to get away from the fact that Apollo 11 is dominating the news right now. Even Pravda in Russia is now headlining the mission and calls Neil Armstrong, "the Czar of the Ship".

Bruce McCandless @BMCAPCOM
West Germany is declaring Monday to be 'Apollo Day.' Schoolchildren in many European countries have been given the day off and large TV sets are being installed in many public places.

Bruce McCandless @BMCAPCOM
The BBC in London is installing a special alarm system to call people to their TVs in case there is a change in the time Neil will open the hatch and climb down to the Moon's surface.

Bruce McCandless @BMCAPCOM
In Italy, Pope Paul VI has arranged for a special color TV circuit at his summer residence so he can watch the Moon landing, even though Italian television is still black and white.

Bruce McCandless @BMCAPCOM
The big news around Houston today concerns the Astros who rallied in the ninth inning to dump the Reds 7 to 4. The Astros had been trailing.

Michael Collins @CMPApollo11
Those Astros have really been catching those flies ever since they put a roof on the stadium.

Bruce McCandless @BMCAPCOM
About to read up roll, pitch and yaw coordinates along with their detailed maneuvering procedures and star alignment coordinates.

Neil Armstrong @CMDRApollo11
The view of the Moon we've been having recently is really spectacular. We're so close now that if fills about three quarters of the hatch window.

Neil Armstrong @CMDRApollo11
We can see the entire circumference, even though part of it is in shadow and part in Earthshine. The view alone is worth the price of the trip.

Bruce McCandless @BMCAPCOM
We observe Apollo 11 maneuvering at this time and will have some updates for them in a couple of minutes.

Buzz Aldrin @LMPApollo11
Bruce is calling again with some updates on the last maneuver. The 'Czar' is brushing his teeth at the moment so I'll fill in for him.

Bruce McCandless @BMCAPCOM
On the basis of Apollo 11's last alignment, the platform looks like it is indeed performing very well. No problems there. None at all. Voice comms are now loud and clear on the high gain antenna.

Bruce McCandless @BMCAPCOM
We need the crew to cycle all the fans in all four CRYO tanks. We want to do this in advance of lunar orbit insertion to ensure, hopefully, that they don't have any MASTER ALARM caution and warning during the insertion burn.

Buzz Aldrin @LMPApollo11
All four CRYO tanks have now been stirred.

Bruce McCandless @BMCAPCOM
We observed Apollo 11's gimbal test down here and it looked good to us.

Neil Armstrong @CMDRApollo11
Alignment and attitude look good to us up here too. Reading Houston loud and clear now.

David Brinkley @DBCABCNews
Apollo 11 is now just 1,000 miles from the Moon and approaching rapidly. Less than 15 minutes from now, the spacecraft will go behind the Moon during which time it will be out of contact with Earth.

David Brinkley @DBCABCNews
While behind the Moon, Neil Armstrong will fire the spacecraft's main engine which will put them into orbit around the Moon.

Jules Bergman @JBABCNews
The burn that will take place behind the Moon will slow down Apollo 11 so that it can be captured by the Moon's gravity. This will be a huge rocket engine burn and will take place about 6 minutes from now.

Jules Bergman @JBABCNews
The burn to slow down Apollo 11 will consume more than 7 tons of fuel. The speed of the combined spacecraft will then be reduced from nearly 6,000 mph to (just!) 3,700 mph.

Jules Bergman @JBABCNews
The reduction in speed should cause the spacecraft to move closer to the Moon, fall if you like, be captured by the Moon's gravity and enter into a stable lunar orbit if all goes well.

Jules Bergman @JBABCNews
Apollo 11 will then circle the Moon 13 times until they are ready to begin the separation and descent procedures and maneuvers ahead of the planned landing tomorrow.

David Brinkley @DBNBCNews
The White House has just announced that President Nixon will talk briefly with astronauts Armstrong and Aldrin while they are actually walking on the Moon's surface. We are unsure as to whether or not the astronauts have been informed of this.

Bruce McCandless @BMCAPCOM
Apollo 11 is now GO for lunar orbit insertion. I'll give them a mark at 13 minutes and 30 seconds to ignition.

Bruce McCandless @BMCAPCOM
Two minutes to the long lunar orbit insertion burn and Apollo 11 is about to disappear around the Moon.

Bruce McCandless @BMCAPCOM
All systems are looking good as Apollo 11 goes around the corner. We'll see them when they emerge on the other side, hopefully having completed the lunar orbit insertion burn..

3 days 4 hours 14 minutes mission time

Bruce McCandless @BMCAPCOM
Apollo should have emerged from behind the Moon at this point. We're trying to re-establish contact.

Bruce McCandless @BMCAPCOM
Still no reply from Apollo 11.

Bruce McCandless @BMCAPCOM
Still no contact.

Buzz Aldrin @LMPApollo11
Back in contact with Houston now! The six-minute burn to bring us down into lunar orbit went fine!

David Brinkley @DBNBCNews
The telemetry and voice signals from Apollo 11 have now been re-acquired as it emerged from behind the Moon. There is a huge amount of clapping and cheering now in Mission Control as many controllers stand up and applaud the astronauts.

Buzz Aldrin @LMPApollo11
We are now in secure lunar orbit and expect to stay in such until about 79 hours 10 minutes.

Bruce McCandless @BMCAPCOM
Okay. We have them now but are reading them very weakly. However, we were able to copy Neil's burn status report and the spacecraft is looking good to us on telemetry.

David Brinkley @DBNBCNews
As Apollo 11 emerges from behind the Moon in a secure orbit, we are hearing that the mysterious Soviet Luna-15 spacecraft has moved into a slightly higher orbit around the Moon.

David Brinkley @DBNBCNews
The Soviets have still not released any details of the ultimate mission of Luna-15, so we don't know if they intend to collect some lunar samples and get back to Earth with them before Apollo 11 can bring back their moonrocks.

Neil Armstrong @CMDRApollo11
We are getting our first view of the landing area. Right now, we are going over the Taruntius crater. The pictures and maps brought back by Apollo 8 and 10 have given us a good preview of what to look for here.

Neil Armstrong @CMDRApollo11
The view looks very much like the pictures, but it's like the difference between watching a real football game and watching on TV. There's no substitute for actually being here.

Buzz Aldrin @LMPApollo11
We're going over the Messier series of craters right now. In Messier A, we can see good-sized blocks in the bottom of the crater. I don't know what our altitude is now, but those are good-sized blocks.

Bruce McCandless @BMCAPCOM
At this time, Apollo 11 is roughly 127 miles above the lunar surface.

Buzz Aldrin @LMPApollo11
We're going over Mount Marilyn now. Down on Earth, Jim Lovell will be smiling right now. He named it for his wife Marilyn.

Bruce McCandless @BMCAPCOM
We have about 6 minutes remaining until the next loss of signal as Apollo 11 goes out of line of sight around the far side of the Moon. We should acquire the signal again at 78 hours 23 minutes 31 seconds.

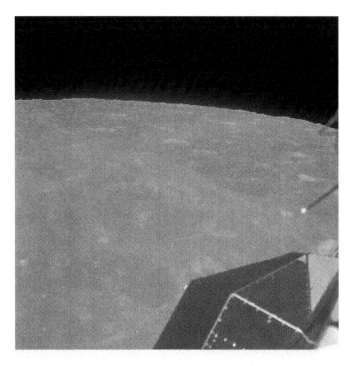

Charlie Duke @CDCAPCOM
We see Apollo 11 at an altitude of about 92 nautical miles above the lunar surface right now.

Michael Collins @CMPApollo11
We are going to move from the side window to the hatch window and we'll try to pick up some of the landmarks that we'll be looking at as we approach the powered descent to the surface.

Charlie Duke @CDCAPCOM
Our instruments show Apollo 11 just southwest of the crater Jansky right now.

Buzz Aldrin @LMPApollo11
We're over Smythe's Sea now. About 88 degrees east.

Neil Armstrong @CMDRApollo11
We're getting close to the point where we will be when we are ready to separate and begin the powered descent in Eagle. The point is equivalent to 13 minutes before ignition.

Charlie Duke @CDCAPCOM
We show the spacecraft now at an altitude of about 110 miles. Of course, they'll be considerably lower at the initiation of powered descent.

Buzz Aldrin @LMPApollo11
We're still sending pictures down and Houston say they're receiving them real clear. I'm about to zoom in on crater Schubert B.

Michael Collins @CMPApollo11
I'm looking at the data on the DSKY (Display and Keyboard). Everything is stabilized now and holding steady.

Charlie Duke @CDCAPCOM
We're receiving a beautiful picture of Langrenus now with its rather conspicuous central peak.

Michael Collins @CMPApollo11
The Sea of Fertility doesn't look very fertile to me. I don't know who named it.

Neil Armstrong @CMDRApollo11
That 'sea' may have been named by the gentleman whom the crater Langrenus was named after – Langrenus. He was a cartographer to the King of Spain and made one of the first reasonably accurate maps of the Moon.

Charlie Duke @CDCAPCOM
Dr. Armstrong is quite the historian on these matters, isn't he?

Neil Armstrong @CMDRApollo11
At least 'Sea of Fertility' sounds much better for the purposes of this mission than 'the Sea of Crisis'. I don't want to go anywhere near that one. 'Sea of Tranquility' sounds much better to me.

Buzz Aldrin @LMPApollo11
In the Sea of Fertility, we are seeing a number of craters that are just barely discernible. Old, old craters whose outlines we can barely see.

Buzz Aldrin @LMPApollo11
We're now getting a good look at what we call Boot Hill. That one occurs 20 seconds into the descent.

Charlie Duke @CDCAPCOM
Current altitude of Apollo 11 is 148 nautical miles above the surface.

Michael Collins @CMPApollo11
I'm unable to determine altitude when looking out of the window. I can't tell whether we are as low as 60 miles or as high as 170 miles.

Charlie Duke @CDCAPCOM
I'll bet any of the crew could tell if they were down at 50,000 feet.

Buzz Aldrin @LMPApollo11
At this point, Neil and I will be 3 minutes and 15 seconds into the descent.

Buzz Aldrin @LMPApollo11
We will conduct a position check at 3 minutes and 39 seconds into the descent. We'll check down range position and cross range position.

Buzz Aldrin @LMPApollo11
We will then yaw over face up to acquire the landing radar. Past this point, we will be unable to see the surface below us until we get very near the landing area.

Michael Collins @CMPApollo11
I think Houston should be getting some good data on my thruster firing versus pitch angle. It looks like that lunar module just wants to head straight down to the lunar surface.

Charlie Duke @CDCAPCOM
Someone here at Mission Control just commented that heading down to the lunar surface is what the lunar module was built to do.

Buzz Aldrin @LMPApollo11
Coming up on the lunar terminator (line of shadow) now.

Michael Collins @CMPApollo11
And as the Moon sinks slowly in the west, Apollo 11 bids farewell to Mission Control and the people of planet Earth.

Charlie Duke @CDCAPCOM
We sort of thought it was the **Sun** sinking in the **east**. Mike Collins says it depends on your point of view.

3 days 6 hours 58 minutes mission time

Charlie Duke @CDCAPCOM
About to read up several pages of star coordinates, orientation and attitude procedures to the crew. All highly technical and numbers-based. Not worth noting down here.

Charlie Duke @CDCAPCOM
Neil and Buzz will start entering lunar module Eagle at about 96 hours. However, if they'd like to initiate this

ingress earlier, we'd like to know so we can call the people in ahead of time.

Philip Gibson @philiplaos
This is gripping stuff! Incredible to think that we have come this far just 66 years after the first manned flight - the Wright brothers' Kitty Hawk - flew for just 12 seconds covering a distance of just 120 feet.

Charlie Duke @CDCAPCOM
Two minutes to next loss of signal as Apollo goes around the far side of the Moon one more time. When they emerge, the White Team CAPCOM will be in my chair.

Michael Collins @CMPApollo11
We're starting our yaw, pitch and roll maneuvers to get into sleep attitude now.

Owen Garriott @OGCAPCOM
We have completed our lunar module systems checks down here and everything looks fine. We've also looked at the results of the landing area tracking. Everything looks fine on that front too.

Owen Garriott @OGCAPCOM
We'd like Apollo 11 to delay the next fuel cell purge until the backside of the Moon, and they need to terminate their battery charge at this time.

Owen Garriott @OGCAPCOM
In order to balance their CRYO tanks, the crew need to get their oxygen tank heater number 1 and hydrogen tank heater number 2 to OFF.

Owen Garriott @OGCAPCOM
We have about 14 minutes to the next loss of signal. Next acquisition of signal is an hour away. Mike Collins has confirmed that there will be at least one crewmember remaining awake during that time.

Neil Armstrong aboard Apollo 11

Neil Armstrong @CMDRApollo11
We are about to depart the command module and enter lunar module Eagle in preparation for descent. We have the command module hatch out, the drogue and probe removed and stowed and we're just about to open the lunar module hatch.

Michael Collins @CMPApollo11
I'm seeing some water inside the command module. There's a little puddle of it on the aft bulkhead.

Buzz Aldrin @LMPApollo11
Neil and I are in lunar module Eagle now and we can clearly see what will be our landing area out of the left window.

Charlie Duke @CDCAPCOM
We have lost all voice and data with command module
Columbia. Only able to communicate with lunar
module Eagle right now.

3 days 21 hours 32 minutes mission time

Ronald Evans @RECAPCOM
Yours truly back in the CAPCOM chair. Apollo 11 is
now 2 minutes away from the next loss of signal as
they pass behind the Moon once more.

Buzz Aldrin @LMPApollo11
We just had another very good view of the landing
site. We were able to pick out most of the features we
had identified earlier.

Ronald Evans @RECAPCOM
The 'Black Bugle' has just arrived with the morning
news briefs. Church services around the world today
are mentioning Apollo 11 in their services. President
Nixon's worship service at the White House is also
dedicated to the mission.

Ronald Evans @RECAPCOM
Frank Borman will read the passage from Genesis
which was read on the Apollo 8 mission last
Christmas. Gloria Diaz of the Philippines was crowned
Miss Universe last night. She has black hair and eyes
and measures 34-23-34.

Ronald Evans @RECAPCOM
We're getting a lot of noise on the loop right now. We
think it's coming from command module Columbia but
we're unable to tell since we can't raise voice with
Mike Collins.

Buzz Aldrin @LMPApollo11
I'll have Mike switch to the high gain antenna. The noise Houston is getting from Columbia is probably the glycol pump humming away in the background.

Buzz Aldrin @LMPApollo11
I'm about to start with the steerable antenna activation. Okay... got a real good lock on now and Houston should be receiving BIOMED data now.

Buzz Aldrin @LMPApollo11
About to begin an ascent battery check on lunar module Eagle.

Ronald Evans @RECAPCOM
We've got Mike in Columbia back now, but we're not getting any BIOMED telemetry from Neil. Lunar module Eagle is about to perform an E-memory dump.

Ronald Evans @RECAPCOM
We have looked at the E-memory and it's a GO. Thirty seconds to loss of signal. Both spacecraft looking good going over the hill.

4 days 2 hours 18 minutes mission time

Charlie Duke @CDCAPCOM
Waiting to re-establish contact with Apollo 11 as it emerges from behind the Moon.

Charlie Duke @CDCAPCOM
Still waiting. We should have re-acquired the signal by this point.

Charlie Duke @CDCAPCOM
Still no signal or voice from either ship. Oh...wait. Here it comes.

Buzz Aldrin @LMPApollo11
Back in touch with Houston. I fed in the recommended angles for the S-band antenna but I couldn't get a lock on because the antenna would be looking through the lunar module in order to reach Earth.

Buzz Aldrin inside lunar Module Eagle

Buzz Aldrin @LMPApollo11
I have initiated and completed the landing gear extension on lunar module Eagle. It looks fine.

Michael Collins @CMPApollo11
We are confirming mountain and crater checkpoints for separation and descent. Checkpoints Diamondback and Sidewinder are impossible to miss. AUTO optics are pointed a little bit north of crater 130.

Charlie Duke @CDCAPCOM
We have given Buzz the GO to begin reaction control system pressurization, but we need to hold off on the checkout until we get the high bit rate.

Charlie Duke @CDCAPCOM
We are seeing a MASTER ALARM. Lots of people here are looking into what it might be right now.

Michael Collins @CMPApollo11
The last optics update worked just fine. The crater I marked on is a small crater down inside crater 130 as described by John Young.

Charlie Duke @CDCAPCOM
The only thing we're missing here is a drift check. After we finish our load, we need the crew to do a drift check with command module Columbia.

Charlie Duke @CDCAPCOM
After the abort guidance system initialization, we will be ready for the reaction control system checkout.

Buzz Aldrin @LMPApollo11
Houston reports that both the alignment and initialization looked good on their instruments.

Michael Collins @CMPApollo11
I'm disabling my roll right now. Now I need Neil or Buzz to give me a call when their reaction control hot fire in Eagle is complete.

Buzz Aldrin @LMPApollo11
Hot fire is complete and Houston says it looked "super". We are all GO.

Buzz Aldrin @LMPApollo11
Mike has confirmed that his thrusters B3 and C4 and radar transponder in the command module are OFF.

Michael Collins @CMPApollo11
B3 and C4 are OFF. Transponder is set to HEATER which is the same as being OFF. I've got my roll jets back on now and will shortly be maneuvering.

4 days 3 hours 25 minutes mission time

Charlie Duke @CDCAPCOM
We are now GO for undocking of the lunar module Eagle from the command and service module Columbia.

Michael Collins @CMPApollo11
Starting a trim maneuver to abort guidance system attitude.

Michael Collins @CMPApollo11
There will be no television of the undocking. I have all my available windows full of cameras and stuff and I'm busy with other things.

Charlie Duke @CDCAPCOM
One minute to loss of signal.

Jules Bergman @JBABCNews
After separation, lunar module Eagle will descend from 60 miles to 50,000 feet (descent orbit insertion maneuver). They will then be at the correct altitude to begin powered descent to the Sea of Tranquility.

David Brinkley @DBNBCNews
We should have confirmation of the separation burn momentarily. The separation burn should have

happened several minutes ago, but we are hearing no confirmation as of yet.

Neil Armstrong @CMDRApollo11
Lunar module Eagle has now successfully undocked from command module Columbia!

Neil Armstrong @CMDRApollo11
The Eagle now has wings. We have separated and I'm ready to start my yaw maneuver.

David Brinkley @DBNBCNews
It has now been confirmed by both Apollo 11 and Mission Control, Houston that the separation maneuver has been completed and went exactly as scheduled.

Charlie Duke @CDCAPCOM
Reading up the detailed coordinates and revised timings to Neil in the now independent lunar module Eagle.

Charlie Duke @CDCAPCOM
Procedures have been received, read back and approved aboard Eagle. On my mark, it will be 9 minutes 30 seconds to descent orbit ignition burn … 3… 2… 1… Mark!

Neil Armstrong @CMDRApollo11
Houston says they've lost all data from Mike and Columbia. Hopefully, it is just a temporary problem.

David Brinkley @DBNBCNews
Apollo 11 is now nearly ready to initiate the descent orbit insertion burn which will take them into a lower orbit from which they can begin the powered descent to the lunar surface.

Charlie Duke @CDCAPCOM
On my mark, 7 minutes to ignition... 3... 2... 1... Mark!

Michael Collins @CMPApollo11
Back in contact with Houston now. Everything is looking real good.

Charlie Duke @CDCAPCOM
Eagle is looking good for ignition to get them to the correct altitude and orbit to begin their descent to the lunar surface. All stations report we are GO at this time.

Michael Collins @CMPApollo11
I've really stabilized here in Columbia now. I haven't burned a thruster in 5 minutes.

Neil Armstrong @CMDRApollo11
Somebody is upside down.

Charlie Duke @CDCAPCOM
One minute to ignition.

Neil Armstrong @CMDRApollo11
Firing in 4… 3… 2… 1… Ignition!

Neil Armstrong @CMDRApollo11
No problem. Engines fired perfectly. The Eagle is now moving farther away from Columbia.

Michael Collins @CMPApollo11
Eagle is moving away and I'm now reading Neil and Buzz as being 0.27 miles out.

Charlie Duke @CDCAPCOM
We have a revised command module rescue procedure ready to read up to Mike in Columbia when he is ready to copy.

Charlie Duke @CDCAPCOM
We also have the latest lunar surface data and landing procedures to read up to Eagle.

Jules Bergman @JBABCNews
Now that Eagle has separated from the command module, there is still the possibility that, should something go wrong with Eagle, Collins could lower Columbia's orbit and dock again with Eagle. This orbital rescue maneuver has been simulated and practiced many times.

Jules Bergman @JBABCNews
Of course, if something goes wrong with Eagle while it is on the surface of the Moon, no rescue will be possible and Mike Collins would have to return home alone. Something we don't like to think about, but some people have had to.

David Brinkley @DBNBCNews
We understand from confidential sources at the White House that, in the event the astronauts are unable to lift off and leave the Moon, a speech to be delivered to the nation by the president has indeed been prepared.

David Brinkley @DBNBCNews
The wording of the speech, we are told, has been agreed between the White House and senior NASA management. However, that eventuality is something we really don't want to think about at this time.

William Safire @WSWhiteHouse
I put a few last-minute touches to the president's speech to the nation should the lunar module fail to lift off, leaving the astronauts stranded and doomed to expire on the lunar surface.

William Safire @WSWhiteHouse
I have sent the speech over to Haldeman for his and the president's approval. Hopefully, the speech will not be needed and its contents will be kept confidential.

William Safire @WSWhiteHouse
As well as the speech, preparations are in place for the president to call the wives of the astronauts prior to the speech and for a pastor to deliver the last rites to the astronauts.

Michael Collins @CMPApollo11
I'm not sure if Eagle has got its tracking light on. I can't see it.

Buzz Aldrin @LMPApollo11
Our tracking light is on, and Eagle's radar is showing us at seven-tenths of a mile out from Mike in the command module.

Charlie Duke @CDCAPCOM
We've just lost contact with the lunar module. We need Mike to signal them to adjust their antenna attitude again.

Buzz Aldrin @LMPApollo11
Okay. Comms are back and holding steady but scratchy. Expecting loss of signal at 101 hours 28 minutes. Next acquisition of signal at 102 hours 16 minutes.

Charlie Duke @CDCAPCOM
Eagle remains GO for descent orbit insertion.

Buzz Aldrin @LMPApollo11
Standing by for the next MARK from Houston.

Charlie Duke @CDCAPCOM
MARK! All systems on both Eagle and Columbia are looking good as they are about to go over the hill. Loss of signal will be in 7 minutes. Ignition for descent orbit insertion will be on the far side of the Moon.

Buzz Aldrin @LMPApollo11
Three minutes to loss of signal.

4 days 6 hours 15 minutes mission time

Charlie Duke @CDCAPCOM
Mike Collins in the command module reports everything went "swimmingly" around the dark side of

the Moon. Waiting now to hear from lunar module Eagle.

Charlie Duke @CDCAPCOM
We've lost all data telemetry from lunar module Eagle. We need Mike to have them adjust and re-acquire on the high-gain antenna again.

Buzz Aldrin @LMPApollo11
We have re-acquired the high-gain antenna and have reported to Houston that the descent orbit insertion burn was on time and went perfectly.

Charlie Duke @CDCAPCOM
Oh, boy! Lost contact with Eagle again. Mike needs to have them try another time to adjust and re-acquire on the high-gain antenna.

Charlie Duke @CDCAPCOM
Okay. They're back.

Buzz Aldrin @LMPApollo11
I don't know what the problem was there. We just started oscillating around in yaw for no apparent reason.

Charlie Duke @CDCAPCOM
We've looked at the abort guidance system initialization and it looks fine to us down here.

Neil Armstrong @CMDRApollo11
Our radar checks aboard Eagle indicate we are now just 50,000 feet above the lunar surface at our nearest orbital pass over. Our visual altitude checks are steadying out at about 53,000 feet.

Charlie Duke @CDCAPCOM
We are advising Eagle to yaw over to the right to enable us to gain signal strength which is weakening again.

Walter Cronkite @WCCBSNews.
We are now just 14 minutes away from the landing on the Moon should everything continue to go as planned. Gene Kranz is about to poll the room at Mission Control for a GO/NO GO status on whether Eagle can begin its powered descent to the lunar surface.

Charlie Duke @CDCAPCOM
We got Eagle back briefly, but then lost it again on the high-gain antenna. We are relying on Mike Collins in the command module to relay our instructions at the moment.

Charlie Duke @CDCAPCOM
We are back up on the high-gain antenna. On my MARK it will be 3 minutes 30 seconds to ignition for powered descent.

Charlie Duke @CDCAPCOM
MARK!

Charlie Duke @CDCAPCOM
Just under two minutes 30 seconds until ignition for powered descent to the lunar surface.

Buzz Aldrin @LMPApollo11
We have four jets in balanced configuration. Throttle is on minimum. We have reset abort stage. Reset attitude control. Sequence camera coming on now.

Eugene F. Kranz (1933 -)

Gene Kranz graduated from Parks College of St. Louis, Missouri, with a BS in Aeronautical Engineering. After entering the Air Force and serving in South Korea, Kranz began work for McDonnell Aircraft testing missile launches off of B-52s at Holloman Air Force Base. In 1960, he joined the newly-formed Space Task Group at NASA's Langley Research Center in Hampton, Virgina. From 1960 to 1964, Kranz worked in the Flight Control Operations Branch developing and writing rules used by flight directors during manned space flight missions.

When the Manned Spacecraft Center opened in Houston (now the Johnson Space Center), Kranz moved to Texas and became chief of the Flight Control Operations Branch. In Houston, he served as Gemini flight director from 1964 to 1968. He was flight director for the first lunar landing (Apollo 11); and flight director for the return of the Apollo 13 crew. He also served as the flight operations director during the Skylab program from 1969 to 1974.

Charlie Duke @CDCAPCOM
If Buzz aboard Eagle is able to read us, they are now GO for powered descent.

Michael Collins @CMPApollo11
I have relayed to Neil and Buzz onboard Eagle that they are GO for powered descent to the lunar surface and they have confirmed.

Gene Kranz @GKFlgtApollo11
Thirty seconds to ignition for powered descent. All controllers report a GO.

Walter Cronkite @WCCBSNews.
30 seconds to ignition to begin the descent to the Moon. Oh, boy – these affairs are hard on the heart.

Charlie Duke @CDCAPCOM
We've lost them again. They need to go to aft OMNI antenna. Mike Collins has relayed that request.

Buzz Aldrin @LMPApollo11
Burning engines! Commencing powered descent to the lunar surface!

Charlie Duke @CDCAPCOM
We have them back again. Everything is looking good right now. Hoping to maintain contact during the rest of the descent.

Neil Armstrong @CMDRApollo11
Descent looking good so far. Altitude 46,000 feet. Continuing to descend.

Walter Cronkite @WCCBSNews.
Ten minutes to touchdown. Oh, boy! Ten minutes to a landing on the Moon!

Charlie Duke @CDCAPCOM
We show altitude now at 47,000 feet as Eagle continues to descend to the lunar surface.

Buzz Aldrin @LMPApollo11
I'm getting some fluctuation in the AC voltage now.

Charlie Duke @CDCAPCOM
AC fluctuation could be just a meter issue. They're still looking good to us. Coming up on 3 minutes into the powered descent now.

Walter Cronkite @WCCBSNews.
About 4 minutes from now, they will get their first look at the landing area. They are face-down in Eagle, their feet forward, looking through the window to get their bearings.

Walter Cronkite @WCCBSNews.
Now they are shifting to more of an upright position so they can look forward out of the window for their landing site. At this point, they are about three and a half miles high.

Neil Armstrong @CMDRApollo11
Our position checks downrange have us coming in a little long.

Charlie Duke @CDCAPCOM
We have data dropout, but Eagle is still looking good.

Gene Kranz @GKFlgtApollo11
Thirty seconds to next GO/NO GO.

Gene Kranz @GKFlgtApollo11
TELECOM reports loss of signal on lunar module downlink!

Gene Kranz @GKFlgtApollo11
I'm going to go round the horn for GO/NO GO. With no new data, flight controllers need to make their GO/NO GOs based on the data they had prior to loss of signal.

Gene Kranz @GKFlgtApollo11
I have surveyed the room and all controllers report Eagle is GO to continue powered descent.

Walter Cronkite @WCCBSNews.
That GO to continue powered descent is another major milestone passed. They could have aborted the landing at that point if the room had come in with a NO GO decision.

Walter Cronkite @WCCBSNews.
About 58 miles and seven minutes to go before landing.

Neil Armstrong @CMDRApollo11
We have a PROGRAM ALARM inside Eagle... a 1202!

Charlie Duke @CDCAPCOM
Eagle is reporting a 1202 PROGRAM ALARM.

Gene Kranz @GKFlgtApollo11
The PROGRAM ALARM is probably nothing. Everything looks good to us down here and we have got data back. We remain GO at that alarm.

Gene Kranz @GKFlgtApollo11
All flight controllers need to hang tight. We should be throttling down pretty shortly.

Neil Armstrong @CMDRApollo11
We are throttling down at 6 minutes 25 seconds.

Buzz Aldrin @LMPApollo11
Throttle down was on time and went better than in the simulator.

Buzz Aldrin @LMPApollo11
PROGRAM ALARM just went off again.

Gene Kranz @GKFlgtApollo11
We are monitoring PROGRAM ALARMs. We remain at GO. Altitude 27,000 feet.

Buzz Aldrin @LMPApollo11
Houston may tend to lose data again as we gradually pitch over. I'll try AUTO again and see what happens.

Charlie Duke @CDCAPCOM
We're still getting good data from Eagle. They should switch descent engine fuel to MONITOR at this time.

Walter Cronkite @WCCBSNews
Oh, boy!

Charlie Duke @CDCAPCOM
Still looking good. Coming up on 8 minutes 30 seconds into descent... Nine minutes now. Looking great! At 4 minutes to touchdown now. Velocity just 760 feet per second.

Thousands gather in New York's Central Park to watch the landing on giant TV screens

Wally Shirra @WSNASA
760 feet per second on the way down. That is pretty slow for space flight.

Walter Cronkite @WCCBSNews
760 feet per second is the slowest man has ever flown in space. They are now just 1.48 miles high, a little over 5 miles from the landing site and they can pitch forward more now and get a much better view of where they are going.

Charlie Duke @CDCAPCOM
At 7 minutes into powered descent, Eagle is looking great to us.

Buzz Aldrin @LMPApollo11
Okay, looks like it's holding.

Gene Kranz @GKFlgtApollo11
Everybody hang tight. Seven and half minutes.

Neil Armstrong @CMDRApollo11
Manual attitude is good.

Gene Kranz @GKFlgtApollo11
Descent fuel 2 critical!

Buzz Aldrin @LMPApollo11
Monitoring descent Fuel 2.

Gene Kranz @GKFlgtApollo11
Twenty seconds to GO/NO GO for landing.

Gene Kranz @GKFlgtApollo11
RETRO, FIDO and GUIDANCE are GO. CONTROL, TELECOM and GNC are GO!

Gene Kranz @GKFlgtApollo11
EECOM and SURGEON are GO. Eagle is GO for landing!

Charlie Duke @CDCAPCOM
Gene has polled the room and all flight controllers report Eagle is now GO for landing!

Walter Cronkite @WCCBSNews
Oh, boy!

Neil Armstrong @CMDRApollo11
We have another PROGRAM ALARM.

Gene Kranz @GKFlgtApollo11
It's the same type of alarm. Neil can ignore the PROGRAM ALARMS. Eagle remains GO for landing at this time.

Neil Armstrong @CMDRApollo11
Two thousand feet, 47 degrees.

Charlie Duke @CDCAPCOM
Altitude 1,600 feet. Things are looking great. They remain GO.

Neil Armstrong @CMDRApollo11
Seven hundred feet, 33 degrees.

Neil Armstrong @CMDRApollo11
600 feet... 540 feet.

Gene Kranz @GKFlgtApollo11
We're staying quiet now. The only call outs from now on will be on fuel status.

Neil Armstrong @CMDRApollo11
400 feet... 350 feet. We're pegged on horizontal velocity.

Buzz Aldrin @LMPApollo11
220 feet... Neil needs to watch our shadow out there.

Buzz Aldrin @LMPApollo11
Still moving forward and coming down nicely.

Buzz Aldrin @LMPApollo11
120 feet... 100 feet.

Bob Carlton @BCCONTROLApollo11
Fuel critical! Sixty seconds of fuel left.

Walter Cronkite @WCCBSNews
The Eagle is supposed to land with 10 minutes of fuel remaining. 30 seconds is expected to be the point at which they will have to abort the landing.

Charlie Duke @CDCAPCOM
Eagle is at 60 feet and 60 seconds left on fuel.

Neil Armstrong @CMDRApollo11
Computer is acting up. I am going to full manual control.

Neil Armstrong @CMDRApollo11
Designated landing area is no good – too many boulders. I'm flying on, searching for a better spot to touch down in.

Buzz Aldrin @LMPApollo11
I have switched the lights on. Continuing to move forward.

Buzz Aldrin @LMPApollo11
Forward. 40 feet. Kicking up some dust.

Bob Carlton @BCCONTROLApollo11
Only 30 seconds left on fuel!

Buzz Aldrin @LMPApollo11
30 feet. Faint shadow. Forward. We're drifting to the right a little.

Neil Armstrong @CMDRApollo11
Okay. This spot should do. Moving in to set us down.

Bob Carlton @BCCONTROLApollo11
Only 15 seconds left on fuel!

Buzz Aldrin @LMPApollo11
CONTACT LIGHT! Engine stop! Descent engine command override OFF.

Bob Carlton @BCCONTROLApollo11
We see engine shutdown!

Charlie Duke @CDCAPCOM
We copied them down!!!

Neil Armstrong @CMDRApollo11
We are now reporting from Tranquility Base. The Eagle has landed!

Charlie Duke @CDCAPCOM
We are copying Eagle on the ground. They had a bunch of guys about to turn blue down here. We're breathing again.

Walter Cronkite @WCCBSNews
Man on the Moon!!! Oh, boy!

Walter Cronkite @WCCBSNews
I had to ask Wally to say something to the TV viewers. I'm stupefied and not a little teared-up here, as is Wally Schirra sitting next to me and most of the guys in our TV studio here.

Michael Collins @CMPApollo11
I heard the whole thing. Fantastic show! Good thing Houston put me on relay. I was missing all the action.

Walter Cronkite @WCCBSNews
The low fuel indicator had them at 60 seconds remaining, then only 30 seconds remaining and they landed with only 15 seconds-worth of fuel remaining. Whew!

Wally Shirra @WSNASA
They found a good landing spot just in time and came darn close to having to abort.

Charlie Duke @CDCAPCOM
We are advising Tranquility Base that there are a lot of smiling faces here in Houston... and all over the world! That was a beautiful job those guys did!

Gene Kranz @GKFlgtApollo11
We need to CUT DOWN ON ALL THE CHATTER in this room and CALM DOWN! Work to do! We are 30 seconds away from STAY/NO STAY flight controllers' reports.

Neil Armstrong @CMDRApollo11
So, we're here. On the Moon. After Buzz shut down the engines, we allowed ourselves a brief celebratory handshake at having made it this far. Now it's back to work. Lots to do.

Gene Kranz @GKFlgtApollo11
All flight controllers have reported in and we are STAY for T1.

Michael Collins @CMPApollo11
I'm asking Houston not to forget the lonely guy circling overhead in command module Columbia while they're handing out all these plaudits to the Eagle crew.

Neil Armstrong @CMDRApollo11
I heard Mike's comments to Houston, and he's right. As command module pilot, he deserves just as much recognition for a successful landing as Buzz and I do. Indeed, it was the whole NASA team that succeeded here.

Neil Armstrong @CMDRApollo11
I've asked Mike to keep that orbiting base ready and shipshape for our return and he assured me he will.

Neil Armstrong @CMDRApollo11
That may have seemed like a very long final phase of the landing, but the AUTO targeting was taking us right into a football field-sized crater with a large number of big boulders the size of cars and lots of other rocks strewn about.

Neil Armstrong @CMDRApollo11
I decided to fly on manually over the rock field to find a reasonably good alternate landing area. Sorry if I gave everyone heart palpitations back in Houston.

Buzz Aldrin @LMPApollo11
Okay. I'm going to be busy for a while here, but that was a very smooth touchdown. I'm venting the oxidizer now.

Walter Cronkite @WCCBSNews
There is now a nine-minute period they have in which they could, under certain emergency conditions take off again and, within two orbits, re-rendezvous with Mike Collins in the command module.

Charlie Duke @CDCAPCOM
We have an unofficial time for the touchdown at 102 hours 45 minutes 42 seconds.

Neil Armstrong @CMDRApollo11
Looking outside, I can see rocks of just about every variety of shape, angularity and granularity. There doesn't appear to be too much of any general color at all.

Buzz Aldrin @LMPApollo11
We are now in one-sixth gravity and it feels just like in the specialized airplane during training.

Neil Armstrong @CMDRApollo11
We don't notice any difficulty at all in adapting to one-sixth gravity. It feels immediately natural to move in this environment.

Charlie Duke @CDCAPCOM
All the consumables on Eagle are solid, and we copy their venting of the descent propulsion system. Everything is copasetic at this point.

Philip Gibson @philiplaos
Copasetic? That's a new one for me. Had to look it up. Here I am trying to qualify as an English teacher and still having to look up words. Never mind – this experience has been well worth staying up for. What a thing this is!

Neil Armstrong @CMDRApollo11
The guys who said we wouldn't be able to tell where we are after landing are the winners today. Aside from a good look at the craters we came over during descent, I haven't been able to pick out the known landmarks on the horizon as a reference yet.

Neil Armstrong @CMDRApollo11
In the final stages of the descent, when we would optimally be carefully identifying the area, we were pretty busy worrying about PROGRAM ALARMS and things like that.

Charlie Duke @CDCAPCOM
Neil doesn't need to concern himself with where they are. We'll figure that out for them.

David Brinkley @DBNBCNews
So now we have Tranquility Base – a new word, a new name and a new place in the Solar System. Also, the beginning of a new frontier – the gateway to Mars.

David Brinkley @DBNBCNews
We are told that President Nixon watched the touchdown on the Moon on a portable television set in the Oval Office.

David Brinkley @DBNBCNews
We are showing our viewers the flight of Eagle to the landing site on our 'telestrator'. The telestrator is an amazing new electronic device which enables us to electronically write on a television screen.

David Brinkley @DBNBCNews
None of the astronauts involved in this historic and very dangerous operation is soon to become a millionaire as a result of this mission. When asked

what he will do after this mission, Buzz Aldrin replied, "Well, I'm not going to become a millionaire."

David Brinkley @DBNBCNews
I guess it's a good thing they have other motivations. Neil Armstrong gets about $30,000 a year. He is a civilian of course. Colonel Aldrin gets around $18,000, and Lieutenant Colonel Collins about $17,500 a year.

David Brinkley @DBNBCNews
However, there is somebody who is going to make more from this landing than most astronauts will make in a year. A 26-year-old Englishman made a bet 5 years ago that a man would land on the Moon before 1971.

David Brinkley @DBNBCNews
The man, David Troufall, a science fiction buff, took odds of 1,000-1 from one of England's largest bookmakers, William Hill, and now is looking at a $24,000 payout.

David Troufall @DTroufall
I started to believe I would win the bet in 1966 when NASA proved they could do an unmanned soft landing on the Moon, proving the Moon wasn't made of green cheese or what have you. Since then, I've been growing in confidence year by year with each successive mission.

Jules Bergman @JBABCNews
Five years ago, I would say odds of 1,000-1 were not realistic considering where we were at in the program at that time. 100-1 maybe. Or 10-1 more likely. Sure wish I had known about those odds and been in England back then.

David Brinkley @DBNBCNews
I actually have a reservation for a flight to the Moon as a paying passenger, although I haven't paid anything yet. It's issued by Pan-Am and more than 17,000 persons have already applied to Pan-Am for a Moon ticket.

David Brinkley @DBNBCNews
Whole families have applied for seats on the first flights, despite the estimated round-trip fare of $28,000 per person. Pan-Am doesn't make any promises, but notes that commercial aviation is never very far behind scientific pioneering.

David Brinkley @DBNBCNews
Perhaps one of those first commercial Moon flights is something that lucky young man in England, a science fiction enthusiast himself, might consider spending his NASA-provided windfall on. He'd better be quick – after today's successful landing, I expect there'll be a rush for reservations.

Neil Armstrong @CMDRApollo11
The area out of the left hand window is a relatively level plain with a fairly large number of craters of the 5 to 50 foot variety and some small 20-30 foot ridges.

Neil Armstrong @CMDRApollo11
There are literally thousands of little 1 and 2 foot craters around the area. I can see fair-sized blocks several hundred feet in front of us that are probably 2 feet in size and have angular edges.

Neil Armstrong @CMDRApollo11
There is a hill in view, just about on the ground track ahead of us. Difficult to estimate, but it might be half a mile or a mile.

Michael Collins @CMPApollo11
Looks like the designated landing area was a NO-GO as far as Neil was concerned.

Neil Armstrong @CMDRApollo11
The targeted landing area was extremely rough, cratered and large numbers of rocks, many larger than 5 to 10 feet in size.

Michael Collins @CMPApollo11
I guess Neil's motto is, "When in doubt, land long."

Charlie Duke @CDCAPCOM
Landing long is certainly what Neil did. Damn near caused a few seizures here in Mission Control. He landed with less than 15 seconds of descent fuel left.

Michael Collins @CMPApollo11
Houston are trying to give me some indication of where Eagle landed, but they don't have a real good handle on it yet. They know it landed long, but are unsure if it touched down left or right of the center line.

Charlie Duke @CDCAPCOM
Neil is reporting Eagle's mission timer has stopped recording time and is frozen at a previous reading. We have some guys researching the problem.

Neil Armstrong @CMDRApollo11
Out of my overhead hatch, I'm looking directly at the Earth. It's big and bright and beautiful. Buzz is going to have a try at identifying some stars through the optics.

Charlie Duke @CDCAPCOM
Two minutes to next loss of signal from Columbia.
Mike is still looking great as he goes over the hill.
Since Eagle's mission timer is down, we'll be giving
them a hack on elapsed mission time every 30
minutes to keep them straight.

Buzz Aldrin @LMPApollo11
We have a PROGRAM ALARM going off in lunar module
Eagle right now.

Charlie Duke @CDCAPCOM
We have people looking into what might have caused
this latest PROGRAM ALARM. It must get really
annoying, and not a little scary, for those guys up
there on the lunar surface. Hope the view
compensates.

Neil Armstrong @CMDRApollo11
We have now read back and confirmed our
understanding of the latest lengthy batch of technical
updates from Houston. Now handing back the display
and keyboard to Mission Control.

Charlie Duke @CDCAPCOM
We now estimate lunar module Eagle landed about 4
miles downrange from the designated landing area.
We'll have a map location up to to Mike Collins in the
command module shortly.

Neil Armstrong @CMDRApollo11
We're suddenly getting a good-sized battery difference
between battery volts on 5 and 6. I don't know if that
is a potential problem or not. Waiting for Houston.

Jules Bergman @JBABCNews
We are waiting for Houston to run the next series of STAY/NO STAY checks. One of the concerns right now is the temperature on the Moon which is extremely hot – way above boiling point. The concern is that the intense heat could affect fluids inside the spacecraft's systems.

Jules Bergman @JBABCNews
If the conclusion is NO STAY, the astronauts will have to lift off from the lunar surface immediately, thus aborting the planned extra vehicular activity (the walk on the Moon).

Charlie Duke @CDCAPCOM
We've looked at the battery issue on lunar module Eagle and conclude that it is not a problem at this stage. Mission is still a GO.

Charlie Duke @CDCAPCOM
Tranquility Base can start the scheduled powerdown now. White Team is going off and letting the Maroon Team take over at this time. We sure appreciate the great show and the beautiful job those guys did up there today.

Buzz Aldrin @LMPApollo11
Neil and I are recommending to Houston that we begin our exit from Eagle onto the lunar surface early starting at about 8 o'clock this evening. That's about 3 hours from now.

Bruce McCandless @BMCAPCOM
Buzz gave us some time to think about an early EVA (extra vehicular activity). We have thought about it and support it. Neil is a GO to exit Eagle and step onto the lunar surface at that time – 3 hours from now.

Bruce McCandless @BMCAPCOM
However, we need to know if that time relates to hatch opening or to preparations for the EVA.

Buzz Aldrin @LMPApollo11
The 3 hours from now time to begin the EVA refers to us opening the hatch on lunar module Eagle. We will begin preparations in about one hour from now.

Michael Collins @CMPApollo11
I'm not able to pick out lunar module Eagle on the Moon's surface. I just picked out a distinguishable crater close to the coordinates Houston sent me and marked it for reference on my next time around.

Michael Collins @CMPApollo11
It looks a nice area though.

Bruce McCandless @BMCAPCOM
Our venting and fuel problem has been cleared up. We are in good shape now. However, we noticed Columbia is maneuvering very close to gimbal lock and have advised Mike to move away.

Michael Collins @CMPApollo11
There are three gimbals to contend with here, so it's pretty tricky. I've asked Houston if they could send me a fourth gimbal for Christmas.

Michael Collins @CMPApollo11
Houston just told me that Neil will be climbing down to the lunar surface at 108 hours mission time. Four hours earlier than planned. Still, they will have time for some lunch before setting off on their EVA.

Bruce McCandless @BMCAPCOM
We've reviewed the checklist, and the only change needed in order to bring forward the timing of the EVA is to delay the lithium hydroxide canister change until after the EVA.

Buzz Aldrin @LMPApollo11
As lunar module pilot, I would like to ask everyone back on Earth, whoever and wherever they may be, at this time, to pause for a moment and contemplate the events of the past few hours and give thanks in his or her own way.

Michael Collins @CMPApollo11
I'm coming up for my next pass over the landing site and hoping I'll be able to see lunar module Eagle. I've asked Houston to send me any topographical data that may help me do so.

Bruce McCandless @BMCAPCOM
The best topographical advice we can give Mike to help him spot Eagle is to look to the west of the irregularly-shaped crater when it comes into view and then work down to the southwest of it.

Michael Collins @CMPApollo11
Last time around, I kept my eyes glues to the sextant hoping I'd get a flash of reflected light off the lunar module but couldn't catch anything. No sign of Eagle on the lunar surface.

Neil Armstrong @CMDRApollo11
Inside lunar module Eagle, we have finished eating and are beginning our preparations for the EVA.

Bruce McCandless @BMCAPCOM
We believe Mike was looking a little too far west and south. Hopefully, he will have better luck at spotting Eagle on the next pass over.

Bruce McCandless @BMCAPCOM
Neil and Buzz have now confirmed that they are at the top of page 27 of the surface checklist in preparation for the EVA onto the lunar surface.

Michael Collins @CMPApollo11
I haven't heard a word from Eagle. I thought I'd be hearing from them on the S-band relay.

Bruce McCandless @BMCAPCOM
We're working on giving Columbia a partial relay so Mike can monitor transmissions from Neil and Buzz at Tranquility Base. It wouldn't do for him to feel out of touch while he continues to circle the Moon.

Bruce McCandless @BMCAPCOM
Mike is approximately 2 minutes to next loss of signal as he passes behind the Moon. All systems on Columbia are looking good. Hopefully, we'll have the partial relay uplinked by the time he re-emerges.

Neil Armstrong @CMDRApollo11
We are continuing to work our way through the checklist in preparation for the EVA. Currently in the middle of page 28.

Bruce McCandless @BMCAPCOM
The crew of Eagle have completed the EVA checklist and are now donning their PLSS (Portable Life Support Systems) – what regular people might call 'spacesuits'.

Bruce McCandless @BMCAPCOM
Buzz now has his PLSS on and Neil is checking the comms on his. We're reading both of them loud and clear right now.

Neil Armstrong @CMDRApollo11
Looking at our tiny TV monitor here, it looks like when I exit the lunar module, Houston will see the area around the ladder in complete dark shadow, but I'm sure they will get a picture from the lighted horizon.

Michael Collins @CMPApollo11
I'm reading Tranquility Base on the relay now, but it's breaking up. Up until about 3 minutes ago, I was reading them loud and clear.

Bruce McCandless @BMCAPCOM
Tranquility Base is now GO for cabin depressurization in advance of exiting the lunar module and stepping onto the Moon.

Buzz Aldrin @LMPApollo11
I am setting suit gas diverter valve to EGRESS. Uh, oh. We just got a MASTER ALARM.

Neil Armstrong @CMDRApollo11
Following the MASTER ALARM, the environmental control system caution light and water separation lights are both ON. Maybe it takes a while for the water separator.

Buzz Aldrin @LMPApollo11
I don't understand. Suit number 1 circuit breaker opened.

Neil Armstrong @CMDRApollo11
Alarm was due to the water separator. We're putting both suit isolator valves to SUIT DISCONNECT.

Neil Armstrong @CMDRApollo11
Now disconnecting lunar module hoses.

Buzz Aldrin @LMPApollo11
Purge valves are now locked and double locked. Nearly set to step out onto the lunar surface. These could be historic TV moments. Sure wish I had shaved last night.

Neil Armstrong @CMDRApollo11
Helmets are now locked and aligned.

Buzz Aldrin @LMPApollo11
Water hoses to our suits are connected. Blue locks are checked. Red locks are checked. Purge locks, water locks and comms are checked.

Neil Armstrong @CMDRApollo11
My portable PLSS is on, with all systems connected and running.

Buzz Aldrin @LMPApollo11
My PLSS is running too, and it's cooling already.

Buzz Aldrin @LMPApollo11
Gloves are on and locked. We are now fully suited up, with all systems connected and we are ready to go and have a look around outside.

NOTE FROM THE AUTHOR:

Philip Gibson @philiplaos

If you are wondering how the astronauts can make these posts while in their bulky spacesuits and gloves, please imagine that they are doing so using a voice to text messaging system.

Neil Armstrong @CMDRApollo11
Cabin pressure is moving towards zero. Suit circuit pressure is 36 to 43. Ready to open the hatch when cabin pressure reaches zero.

Buzz Aldrin @LMPApollo11
Cabin pressure is now down to 0.2. Sure takes a long time to get all the way down.

Buzz Aldrin @LMPApollo11
I have unlocked the lunar module hatch. Cabin pressure should be enough about right now to allow us to open the hatch. I'll give it a try.

Neil Armstrong @CMDRApollo11
Cabin pressure is now 0.1. The hatch should pop open smoothly at this pressure level.

Neil Armstrong @CMDRApollo11
The hatch is coming open.

Walter Cronkite @WCCBSNews
The 2 hours and 40 minutes of the walk on the Moon begins with the hatch opening. Here we go!

Buzz Aldrin @LMPApollo11
I'm holding the hatch door from going back into the closed position. Waiting for Neil. We are about ready to go down and get some moon rocks.

Neil Armstrong @CMDRApollo11
Okay. Now for the gymnastics.

Neil Armstrong @CMDRApollo11
I'm on the porch now. Buzz is guiding me regarding my left and right feet positions and keeping me away from snagging anything on my suit as I exit Eagle.

Buzz Aldrin @LMPApollo11
Okay. Neil is nice and straight now, but I need to pull the hatch open a little more.

Buzz Aldrin @LMPApollo11
Done... Neil is now exiting lunar module Eagle and about to climb down the ladder and step onto the Moon.

Bruce McCandless @BMCAPCOM
We are following everything Neil and Buzz are doing on audio right now and waiting for their TV.

Buzz Aldrin @LMPApollo11
TV circuit breaker is in. Houston should be getting live pictures now.

Bruce McCandless @BMCAPCOM
Okay. We have TV coming down now. We can see the ladder extending from the lunar module to the lunar surface.

Neil Armstrong @CMDRApollo11
Taking great care maneuvering while exiting the lunar module. There's very little clearance and it would very easy to snag some of my gear around or above the hatch.

Bruce McCandless @BMCAPCOM
There's a great deal of contrast in the picture and currently it's upside down on our monitor and grainy, but we can make out a fair amount of detail.

Walter Cronkite @WCCBSNews
Okay. They've turned the TV picture the right way up now.

Bruce McCandless @BMCAPCOM
We can see Neil coming down the ladder now. He has nine steps to go before he sets foot on the lunar soil.

Neil Armstrong @CMDRApollo11
Climbing down the ladder... very slowly.

Neil Armstrong @CMDRApollo11
I'm at the foot of the ladder now, about to step onto the Moon. The last step is a bit unstable but still usable.

Neil Armstrong @CMDRApollo11
I'm looking at the lunar module footpads which are only depressed into the surface about one or two inches.

Neil Armstrong @CMDRApollo11
The surface appears to be very, very fine-grained as you get close to it. It's almost like a powder.

Neil Armstrong @CMDRApollo11
Okay. I'm going to step off the lunar module now.

Neil Armstrong @CMDRApollo11
This is one small step for (a) man, one giant leap for mankind.

Walter Cronkite @WCCBSNews
Armstrong is on the Moon! He is standing on the surface of the Moon! And though the TV picture is pretty grainy, we can see that he is indeed standing on the surface of the Moon.

Walter Cronkite @WCCBSNews
Oh, boy!

Philip Gibson @philiplaos
Oh, man! They did it!

Walter Cronkite @WCCBSNews
Just look at those pictures! Neil Armstrong, a 38-year-American, is standing on the surface of the Moon. Incredible!

Jules Bergman @JBABCNews
What a moment! Neil Armstrong has stepped off the ladder and onto the surface of the Moon!

David Brinkley @DBNBCNews
Everyone in our studio is standing up and cheering at the top of their voices. Same thing in Central Park and in Mission Control, Houston.

Neil Armstrong @CMDRApollo11
The surface is so fine and powdery I can pick it up loosely with my toe. It adheres like powdered charcoal to the sole and sides of my boot.

Neil Armstrong @CMDRApollo11
I only go into the surface a small fraction of an inch, maybe an eighth of an inch, but I can see the footprints of my boots and treads in the fine, sandy particles.

Neil Armstrong @CMDRApollo11
There seems to be no difficulty in moving around. It's even easier than the practice we did in various simulations of one-sixth gravity during training.

Neil Armstrong @CMDRApollo11
Eagle's descent engine did not leave a crater of any size. It has about 1 foot clearance on the ground. We're in a very level place here.

Buzz Aldrin @LMPApollo11
Okay. I'll be ready to follow Neil down and exit Eagle myself after I send down the camera so Neil can get a shot of me exiting the lunar module.

Neil Armstrong @CMDRApollo11
I'm in the shadow of Eagle right now and it's a little hard for me to see if I have good footing. I'll make my way over into the sunlight here without looking directly into the Sun.

Bruce McCandless @BMCAPCOM
Unofficial time for man's first step onto the surface of the Moon is 109 hours 24 minutes and 20 seconds elapsed mission time.

Neil Armstrong @CMDRApollo11
I have the camera now. I'll step out a little more and take some of the first pictures from the Moon's surface. From where I am standing now, everything is very clearly visible. The light is very good.

David Brinkley @DBNBCNews
Armstrong now has a camera strapped to his chest. It was delivered to him from the lunar module by a simple clothes line-type system using pulleys operated by both astronauts.

Walter Cronkite @WCCBSNews
Boy, look at Neil Armstrong gingerly bounding around. Looks like he's having fun up there on the Moon.

Bruce McCandless @BMCAPCOM
We are seeing Neil now getting some of the first still pictures. However, we also need him to collect the contingency sample of the lunar surface quickly in case the EVA has to be terminated early.

David Brinkley @DBNBCNews
The contingency sample is number one on the list of scientific priorities – getting that first quick sampling of the lunar soil in case the men have to be brought back early. Mission Control is anxious to get that done quickly.

Walter Cronkite @WCCBSNews
The still pictures Neil Armstrong is taking right now will doubtless be with the very high-quality Hasselblad

camera which has been specially modified for the purpose of this mission.

Neil Armstrong @CMDRApollo11
I'm going to get to collecting the contingency sample as soon as I finish this series of pictures. The light is very good down here. Everything is very clearly visible, including Buzz in the window of the lunar module.

Walter Cronkite @WCCBSNews
I think I recall that the flight plan actually called for the contingency samples to be collected before taking pictures with the still camera. Commander Armstrong may be deviating a little from the flight plan here.

Wally Schirra @WSNASA
It may be that Neil feels that there is no need for contingency operations here – that he has great confidence that they will be able to complete and collect everything they need to complete and collect.

Wally Schirra @WSNASA
Neil has just slipped out of our field of view. I wonder what he's up to now.

Buzz Aldrin @LMPApollo11
Neil is trying to get at the contingency sample, but it looks like it's a little difficult to dig through the initial crust.

Neil Armstrong @CMDRApollo11
This is very interesting. It's a soft surface, but where I plug in with the contingency sample collector, I run into a very hard sub-surface. It appears to be a very cohesive material of some sort. I'll try to pick up a couple of small rocks.

Buzz Aldrin @LMPApollo11
The scene on the ground looks beautiful from up here in Eagle.

Neil Armstrong @CMDRApollo11
It has a stark beauty all its own. It's much like the high desert of the United States. It's actually very pretty out here.

Neil Armstrong @CMDRApollo11
A lot of the rock samples out here have what appear to be vesicles on the surface, and I am looking at one now that appears to have some sort of phenocryst.

Wally Schirra @WSNASA
Neil is describing phenocryst on some of the rocks around him – typical of volcanic rocks.

Buzz Aldrin @LMPApollo11
Okay. Neil says he's ready for me to come out of Eagle now.

Neil Armstrong @CMDRApollo11
Buzz saw the difficulties I was having getting out and climbing down the ladder, so hopefully he'll have an easier time of it. I'll watch his PLSS (portable life support system) from underneath here.

Neil Armstrong @CMDRApollo11
Buzz's toes looked good clearing the sill of the lunar module, although he had just an inch clearance on top of his PLSS getting through the hatch.

Buzz Aldrin @LMPApollo11

Outside the hatch now. Now I need to partially close the hatch, while making sure I don't close it entirely and lock it.

Neil Armstrong @CMDRApollo11
Pretty good thought Buzz had there. The one about not locking us out of the spacecraft. I thoroughly approve of that.

Buzz Aldrin @LMPApollo11
Lunar module Eagle will be our home for the next few hours and we need to take good care of it. So best to close the door like any good homeowner would.

Buzz Aldrin @LMPApollo11
I'm on the top step now and can look down over the landing gear pads. It should be a very simple matter to hop down from one step to the next.

Neil Armstrong @CMDRApollo11
Buzz looks good laterally coming down the ladder. He has three more steps and then the long one off of the slightly-detached final step.

Neil Armstrong @CMDRApollo11
When I got off the ladder, I found hopping down quite easy. Buzz has three more regular steps to go and then the long one... more like a hop with that final step.

David Brinkley @DBNBCNews
That last step is the long one. The reason for that is they really expected, I think, the footpads to push into the lunar soil just a little but further than they did. Buzz Aldrin has now to make a final jump of what looks to be about three feet.

Buzz Aldrin descending from the lunar module

Buzz Aldrin @LMPApollo11
Jumping off the final step now.

Buzz Aldrin @LMPApollo11
Okay! I'm down and standing on the Moon!

Buzz Aldrin @LMPApollo11
I just tried a one-sixth gravity hop up back to the bottom step. Real easy. That was an effortless hop up – about a three-footer.

Buzz Aldrin @LMPApollo11
Hopped back down again. Real easy in this gravity. Turning around. Oh, boy! What a sight! Magnificent desolation! Walking out to join Neil now.

Walter Cronkite @WCCBSNews
Watching the astronauts bouncing around, it looks like they're walking on a trampoline.

Neil Armstrong @CMDRApollo11
I notice that if I kick a clod or small rock, it elevates, spins and then bounces along.

Buzz Aldrin @LMPApollo11
Reaching down is fairly easy, although the backpack does have some effect on inertia. I have already got my suit dirty at this stage.

Buzz Aldrin @LMPApollo11
The mass of the backpack does have some effect on inertia. When I am about to lose my balance in one direction, recovery is quite natural and very easy.

Neil Armstrong @CMDRApollo11
Got to be careful that you are leaning in the direction you want to go, otherwise you seem a bit inebriated. In other words, you have to cross your foot over to stay underneath where your center of mass is.

Buzz Aldrin @LMPApollo11
There's absolutely no crater here at all from the descent engine.

Buzz Aldrin @LMPApollo11
The rocks here seem rather slippery, although traction across the powdery surface seems quite good.

Buzz Aldrin @LMPApollo11
The probes at the bottom of the LEM's landing pads are bent over. One of them has broken off.

Wally Schirra @WSNASA
Those probes are fairly thin, wire-like extensions attached to the bottom of the landing pads. They were there to send a signal to the astronauts when the lunar module was about five feet above the lunar surface.

Walter Cronkite @WCCBSNews
Armstrong is now moving the TV camera out about 30 feet and setting it up on a stand. He'll then point it back at the entire lunar module to get a panoramic view.

Wally Schirra @WSNASA
Uh oh, the picture's inverted again.

Buzz Aldrin @LMPApollo11
I had told Neil earlier that we might see some purple rocks and I think I just have. There are some sparkly fragments. I'd guess some sort of biotite.

Jules Bergman @JBABCNews
I'm being told that the biotite Aldrin is referring to is a brownish, mica substance.

Neil Armstrong @CMDRApollo11
I'm going to change the camera lenses. Houston will tell me if the picture is good or not.

Walter Cronkite @WCCBSNews
They've got three lenses, I believe, along on this flight: a wide-angle 30mm lens, a 90mm lens, and... er... er... another one.

Bruce McCandless @BMCAPCOM
Life support system consumables in the PLSS (portable life support system) suits the astronauts are

wearing are still looking good, as are the systems inside the lunar module.

Bruce McCandless @BMCAPCOM
We're getting a new picture the right way up and we can tell it's a longer focal length lens. We've just had a readout of all the systems aboard lunar module Eagle and they remain GO to remain on the Moon.

Buzz Aldrin @LMPApollo11
Neil is now unveiling the steel plaque we brought to leave behind for posterity. It is attached near the base of Eagle's landing gear.

Neil Armstrong @CMDRApollo11
The plaque shows each of the two hemispheres of the Earth. Underneath it says, "Here men from the planet Earth first set foot upon the Moon, July 1969 AD."

Neil Armstrong @CMDRApollo11
It continues, "We came in peace for all mankind." It has the crewmembers' signatures and the signature of the President of the United States.

Walter Cronkite @WCCBSNews
We can see the space helmeted heads of Armstrong and Aldrin standing in front of the plaque at the base of lunar module Eagle as we listen to those tremendously historic words being read out.

Bruce McCandless @BMCAPCOM
That was quite a moment!

Walter Cronkite @WCCBSNews
When the ascent stage of the lunar module lifts off to
leave the Moon, the descent stage and that historic
metallic plaque will remain on the Moon, perhaps to
be read by future visitors, hundreds or even millions
of years from now.

Bruce McCandless @BMCAPCOM
Neil has moved away from the lunar module now and
is sending down some great images.

Neil Armstrong @CMDRApollo11
I'll move even farther back from Eagle and try to get
some shots with a more panoramic view.

Walter Cronkite @WCCBSNews
We're getting a view over to the horizon as Armstrong
moves that camera. Still very blurry though.

Bruce McCandless @BMCAPCOM
Oh, getting better pictures now! We saw the entire
lunar module for a moment there.

Bruce McCandless @BMCAPCOM
Neil is going a little too fast on the panoramic sweep.
He needs to stop and try it again more slowly.

Neil Armstrong @CMDRApollo11
I'm adjusting a little... about north, north east. I don't
want to go into the Sun if I can avoid it.

Neil Armstrong @CMDRApollo11
Getting a picture right down front, straight west. I need Houston to tell me if they can see an angular rock in the foreground.

Bruce McCandless @BMCAPCOM
We do see the angular rock in the foreground. And it looks like there is a much smaller rock over to the left of it.

Neil Armstrong @CMDRApollo11
Then on beyond, there is a much larger rock that's very rounded. The closest rock is sticking up out of the sand about 1 foot. It's a about a foot and a half long and 6 inches thick, but it's standing on edge.

Bruce McCandless @BMCAPCOM
We can clearly see the long shadows of lunar module Eagle on several of the pictures Neil is sending down.

Neil Armstrong @CMDRApollo11
The little hill just beyond the shadow of the lunar module is a pair of elongate craters. Probably the pair together is about 40 feet long and 20 feet across. Maybe 6 feet deep.

Bruce McCandless @BMCAPCOM
We see Buzz going about his work. He is erecting the solar wind experiment now. He has the table out and the bag deployed.

*Buzz Aldrin captured by the high-quality still camera
as he deploys the solar wind experiment*

Buzz Aldrin @LMPApollo11
I've found I can use the long shadow the staff makes
to see if I have the solar wind experiment
perpendicular or not.

Walter Cronkite @WCCBSNews
Solar wind, of course, is not a 'wind' as we know it on
Earth – something you can feel against your cheeks.
Rather, it is a flow of high-energy electrons and
protons emitted from the Sun at supersonic speeds.

Bruce McCandless @BMCAPCOM
Neil Armstrong has now been on the lunar surface for
45 minutes.

Walter Cronkite @WCCBSNews
These live, black and white, somewhat fuzzy and jerky
TV pictures from the lunar surface remind me of some
of those early science fiction movies of life on the
Moon. They looked just like this.

Bruce McCandless @BMCAPCOM
Mike Collins, circling up above Tranquility Base in the
command ship, just asked us how the EVA is going.
We were able to tell him that it's going "beautifully"
and that they are setting up the flag now.

Bruce McCandless @BMCAPCOM
I guess Mike Collins, while he is orbiting the Moon, is
the only person who does not have TV coverage of the
scene on the Moon's surface right now. Millions are
watching it here on Earth, but there's no TV set inside
command module Columbia.

Neil Armstrong @CMDRApollo11
In the soft spots where we have footprints maybe one
inch deep, the soil is very cohesive and will retain a
slope of around 70 degrees along the side of the
footprints.

Buzz Aldrin @LMPApollo11
Some of these small depressions tend to sink 2 or 3 inches. They suggest exactly what the Surveyor pictures indicated.

Walter Cronkite @WCCBSNews
With no wind or rain to wear those footprints away, they may remain intact for a very long time – possibly millions of years.

Wally Schirra @WSNASA
The intense difference between the intense heat of the lunar day and the intense cold of lunar night would have an erosive effect I would have thought. There had to be some process that created the very fine powdery surface the astronauts are describing.

Buzz Aldrin @LMPApollo11
You get a force transmitted through the surface of the soil and about 5 or 6 inches of bay breaks loose and

moves as if it were caked on the surface, when in fact it really isn't.

Richard Nixon @RNixonPOTUS
My Chief of Staff has informed me that NASA are just about ready for me to speak to our astronauts on the Moon. We're standing by on the telephone to be connected to astronauts Armstrong and Aldrin on the Moon.

Bruce McCandless @BMCAPCOM
They are still setting up the United States flag. Having a little trouble driving it into the lunar surface.

Walter Cronkite @WCCBSNews
Okay, they've got it. There it is! The U.S. flag, the Stars and Stripes, on the surface of the Moon.

Walter Cronkite @WCCBSNews
There is no wind on the Moon of course, so the flag
has a frame of its own to hold it out. Looks great! At
moments like these, it does seem like there should be
some accompanying patriotic music.

Michael Collins @CMPApollo11
I don't mind a bit missing out on the live pictures.
Houston just told me Neil and Buzz have set up the
flag and that they are able to see the stars and stripes
on the lunar surface. Beautiful! Just beautiful!

Walter Cronkite @WCCBSNews
Of course, this planting of the flag is not what it might
have meant in the centuries prior to this one. We are
not claiming the territory for the United States. Not at
all.

Walter Cronkite @WCCBSNews
The Moon cannot be claimed by any country since,
under a United Nations resolution that we signed up
to, the Moon cannot be claimed by any nation, nor be
used by any country for military purposes.

Wally Schirra @WSNASA
I like the idea of not 'claiming' the Moon, but I think
Armstrong and Aldrin can claim it for now at least.

Buzz Aldrin @LMPApollo11
I've saluted the flag along with Neil and am moving
away now. We do have to be careful when walking to
keep track of where our center of mass is. Sometimes,
it takes 2 or 3 paces to make sure we've got our feet
under us.

Buzz Aldrin @LMPApollo11
The so-called 'kangaroo hop' does work, but it seems like our forward mobility is not as good as it is in the more conventional one foot after the other method.

Buzz Aldrin @LMPApollo11
It's hard saying what a sustainable pace might be. I think the rapid one I'm using now might get very tiring after a few hundred yards. But that might be as a function of this suit as well as the lack of gravity.

Richard Nixon @RNixonPOTUS
Still waiting to be connected and speak to Neil and Buzz from the Oval Office in what must certainly be the most historic telephone call ever made from the White House. I have my short speech prepared and ready.

Wally Schirra @WSNASA
Neil and Buzz are now taking color pictures of each other with the high-quality Hasselblad still camera... the first tourists on the Moon, capturing the moment for all time. We will be able to see those high-quality pictures after they are developed back on Earth.

Bruce McCandless @BMCAPCOM
We just got an urgent message direct from the White House and need to get both Neil and Buzz in the field of view of the TV camera right now.

Neil Armstrong @CMDRApollo11
No idea what this is about. Assembling Buzz and I together in front of the camera in this fashion was not called for in the flight plan. Seems like Houston has some kind of surprise in store for us.

Walter Cronkite @WCCBSNews
They've now assembled the two astronauts in front of the TV camera, one on either side of the flag. I think something rather important may be coming up here.

Bruce McCandless @BMCAPCOM
The president is in his office right now, and we are working to patch him through to Tranquility Base on the Moon so he can say a few words to the astronauts. Here we go...

Richard Nixon @RNixonPOTUS
I am now going live to speak to Neil and Buzz on the surface of the Moon.

Richard Nixon @RNixonPOTUS
Hard to express just how proud of these boys we are. For every American, this has to be the proudest day of our lives. And for people all over the world. I'm sure they too will join with Americans in recognizing what an immense feat this is.

Richard Nixon @RNixonPOTUS
Because of what they have done, the heavens have become part of man's world. As they talk to us from the Sea of Tranquility, it inspires us to redouble our efforts to bring peace and tranquility to Earth.

Richard Nixon @RNixonPOTUS
For one priceless moment in the whole history of man, all the people on this Earth are truly one; one in their pride in what these men have done, and one in our prayers that they will return safely to Earth.

Neil Armstrong @CMDRApollo11
Beautiful words indeed from the president. I thanked him and told him it is a great honor and privilege to be

here representing not only the United States, but men of peace of all nations with an interest, curiosity and vision for the future.

Richard Nixon @RNixonPOTUS
In ending my call to Tranquility Base on the surface of the Moon, I thanked the astronauts and told them I look forward to seeing them on the USS Hornet in the Pacific Ocean on Thursday.

Neil Armstrong @CMDRApollo11
The call from the president was quite a surprise. Wonder how long Houston have known about it.

Buzz Aldrin @LMPApollo11
Nice and historic words from the president indeed. Much appreciated. Now back to work. Still much to do in the short time before we leave.

Buzz Aldrin @LMPApollo11
In going from the light to the shadow, I catch an additional reflection of Eagle. I have so much glare coming into my visor, it takes a while to adjust. Inside the shadow area, visibility is not good at all.

Buzz Aldrin @LMPApollo11
The blue color of my boots has completely disappeared now into this kind of ash-cocoa color. It is covering most of the lighter part of my boot with very fine particles. Neil is picking up rocks.

Bruce McCandless @BMCAPCOM
Buzz is cutting out on the end of his transmissions. He needs to speak a little more closely into his microphone.

Buzz Aldrin @LMPApollo11
I can lean forward a little towards the microphone. Hope that helps. In this area, there are two craters. The one in front of me, about 11 o'clock position from the spacecraft, has several boulders 6 to 8 inches across.

Walter Cronkite @WCCBSNews
While Buzz Aldrin is bounding around and Neil Armstrong is collecting his rock samples, we should note that in the Moon's one-sixth gravity, Armstrong weighs only 60 pounds compared to the 360 pounds he weighs on Earth.

Walter Cronkite @WCCBSNews
In addition, the rocks Armstrong is collecting will be weighing one-sixth of what they will weigh when they are brought back to Earth and examined in minute detail in dozens of laboratories around the world.

Neil Armstrong @CMDRApollo11
I've finished collecting the bulk sample of Moon rocks and am sealing the bag now. Some very interesting specimens here to take back to Earth.

Jules Bergman @JBNBCNews
The 50 pounds or so of bulk rock samples Armstrong has collected will be brought back to Earth having been sealed by him in a vacuum and will be opened under vacuum conditions when they arrive in various laboratories around the world back on Earth.

Bruce McCandless @BMCAPCOM
Neil needs to be careful – he's stepping on the TV camera cable. Now he has his foot caught up in it.

Bruce McCandless @BMCAPCOM
Okay, he's unhooked his foot now.

Michael Collins @CMPApollo11
Looking down at the lunar surface from up here the command ship, I'm still unable to pick out the lunar module on the Moon's surface, although I did see a suspiciously small white object at one point. I sent the coordinates down to Houston.

Michael Collins @CMPApollo11
The white object was right on the southwest end of a smallish crater. I think they would know if they were in such a location. It looks like the lunar module would be pitched up quite a bit if that's what it was.

Jules Bergman @JBABCNews
Astronauts Armstrong and Aldrin are now well beyond halfway in their scheduled moonwalk, examination of the lunar module, photography tasks, sample collection and setting up of several experiments on the lunar surface.

Jules Bergman @JBABCNews
Not forgetting the unveiling of the historic plaque to leave on the Moon's surface commemorating the landing, the planting of the U.S. flag in the lunar soil and taking an incredibly historic phone call from the president in the White House.

Jules Bergman @JBABCNews
The seismic experiment, the laser experiment and the solar wind experiment are all 'passive'. They have no moving parts, no power supply. They just sit there. So theoretically, they should last indefinitely.

Bruce McCandless @BMCAPCOM
The flight surgeon has reported that both astronauts on the lunar surface are averaging between 90 and 100 BTU (British Thermal Units) expended in energy of work, right on the predicted number. He says they're in great shape.

Buzz Aldrin @LMPApollo11
The jet deflector that's mounted on quad 4 looks a great deal more wrinkled than the deflector on quad 1. However, the underneath part of the lunar module seems to have stood up quite well to the descent and landing.

Buzz Aldrin looking at one of the deflector pads

Buzz Aldrin @LMPApollo11
It's very surprising looking at the level of penetration of all four of the footpads. If we were to try and determine just how far beneath the surface they have penetrated, I'd say maybe just 3 inches.

Neil Armstrong @CMDRApollo11
I think we can put the lack of penetration of the footpads down to Eagle performing a beautifully soft and guided landing.

Neil Armstrong @CMDRApollo11
Looking at the LEM (lunar excursion module), the pods seem to be in good shape. The primary and secondary struts are in good shape. Antennas are all in place, and there's no evidence of problems underneath the LEM due to engine exhaust or drainage.

Bruce McCandless @BMCAPCOM
Neil and Buzz are now about 30 minutes behind the nominal timeline.

Bruce McCandless @BMCAPCOM
However, we have checked the consumables the astronauts need while outside the lunar module and they're in good shape to continue.

Wally Schirra @WSNASA
Neil and Buzz are having much more motion than we anticipated. They're really romping around up there.

Wally Schirra @WSNASA
It's great to hear the readouts from the critical cooling systems in their portable life support systems (spacesuits) indicating that the suits are performing really well in keeping them cool and supplied with oxygen.

Jules Bergman @JBABCNews
Houston just reported that Neil Armstrong still has 66% of his oxygen remaining, so they are not using up oxygen too fast. That's good to know.

Jules Bergman @JBABCNews
The life support system they are wearing and carrying on their backs utilizes body heat to convert ice into its gaseous state, releasing the oxygen which they are breathing right now.

Neil Armstrong @CMDRApollo11
Fifteen sealed.

Walter Cronkite @WCCBSNews
Armstrong just said "15 sealed". That means he now has 15 rock samples sealed. I guess they've now got about 100 pounds or so of rocks.

Walter Cronkite @WCCBSNews
The astronauts are running about a half hour behind the plan regarding what they will do on the Moon's surface. However, they have completed packing rock samples and Aldrin is now working on the seismometer experiment.

Wally Schirra @WSNASA
The seismometer experiment package includes a seismometer that they will leave on the surface of the Moon that will send back to Earth reports of impacts of meteorites on the Moon's surface as well as any earthquake activity.

Walter Cronkite @WCCBSNews
They will also set up a laser ranging retro reflecting device. That is kind of like a prism-like mirror in order that anyone on Earth with a powerful enough laser will be able to use their laser to focus on the mirror.

Walter Cronkite @WCCBSNews
A lot of people/organizations do have such lasers these days.

Walter Cronkite @WCCBSNews
Those people will then be able to calculate, with the known time and the speed of light and the timed return of that light signal, accurate measurements of the Moon's wobble, the Earth's wobble and even the drifts of the Earth's continents.

Jules Bergman @JBABCNews
These experiments are being set up about 70 feet from the lunar module. The astronauts will be out of the camera's field of view while setting up these experiments.

Buzz Aldrin @LMPApollo11
I have completed manual deployment of the passive seismometer. Wasn't too difficult.

Bruce McCandless @BMCAPCOM
We can see Buzz fairly clearly now through the structure of the minus Z secondary strut of the lunar module.

Walter Cronkite @WCCBSNews
We are hearing from Dan Rather who has been speaking to the White House Press Secretary that, following the successful Moon landing, the president can be expected to soon make a policy decision regarding exploration of the planet Mars.

Walter Cronkite @WCCBSNews
We are told that a presidential decision on a Mars mission will be made within the next 60 days. We have already heard from Vice-President Agnew that he

expects the Space Council to recommend going to Mars.

Neil Armstrong @CMDRApollo11
These boulders look like basalt. They have probably 2% white minerals in them... white crystals. The thing I reported as vesicular before, I no longer think that. Looks more like tiny impact craters, like where birdshot has hit the surface.

Neil Armstrong @CMDRApollo11
The laser reflector is now installed, the bubble is leveled and, after some difficulty, the alignment appears to be good.

Jules Bergman @JBABCNews
The experiments the astronauts are setting up on the Moon will hopefully give us, for years to come, scientifically-useful data about the Moon, the Earth and other heavenly bodies that surround this planet of ours.

Buzz Aldrin @LMPApollo11
As I was spacing the passive seismometer experiment, the right hand solar array deployed automatically. The left hand array I had to bring out manually.

Bruce McCandless @BMCAPCOM
After looking again at consumables, we see them in good shape and subject to their concurrence, we'd like to extend the duration of the EVA 15 minutes beyond nominal.

Bruce McCandless @BMCAPCOM
We will still give Buzz a hack at 10 minutes before heading back into the lunar module. Their current elapsed time is 2 hours and 12 minutes.

Buzz Aldrin @LMPApollo11
An extra quarter of an hour sounds fine. All parts of
the solar array are clear of the ground now.

Bruce McCandless @BMCAPCOM
The passive seismometer experiment has now come
online here in Mission Control and we are already
observing short period oscillations in it.

Bruce McCandless @BMCAPCOM
Neil Armstrong has now been walking on the Moon for
over two hours. Buzz Aldrin is now collecting core tube
samples.

Buzz Aldrin @LMPApollo11
I hope Houston are seeing just how hard I am hammering here into the ground, to the tune of about five inches, to get these core tube samples.

Bruce McCandless @BMCAPCOM
Mike in command ship Columbia has still not been able to spot the lunar module on the surface. Columbia is now one minute away from loss of signal as it passes behind the Moon.

Neil Armstrong @CMDRApollo11
I'm collecting several pieces of really vesicular-looking rock out here now, but I think we don't have enough time to complete all the documented collections.

Jules Bergman @JBABCNews
Now that the astronauts have collected about 100 pounds of Moon rocks, they will compensate for the weight of those rocks in their command module for the return trip home by leaving behind quite an array of equipment.

Jules Bergman @JBABCNews
They'll leave behind the TV equipment, the camera, the tripod, the scientific experiments they have set up, the two portable life support systems and their garments too.

Jules Bergman @JBABCNews
And, of course, the descent stage of the Eagle will also be left behind after they lift off from the lunar surface.

Buzz Aldrin @LMPApollo11
Uh, oh. I've just received the 10 minute notice from Houston to begin EVA termination procedures.

Neil Armstrong @CMDRApollo11
The close-up camera is underneath the modular equipment stowage assembly. I'm having to pick it up with the prong.

Bruce McCandless @BMCAPCOM
Neil and Buzz now have 3 minutes before they should commence EVA termination procedures. No time to collect all the documented samples.

Bruce McCandless @BMCAPCOM
After they have the core tubes and the rock samples, anything else they can throw into the box and send up into Eagle will be acceptable.

Buzz Aldrin @LMPApollo11
Our EVA closeout procedures are now in progress.

Bruce McCandless @BMCAPCOM
Neil needs to get on with getting the close-up camera magazine and closing out the sample return canister. We're running a little low on time.

Buzz Aldrin @LMPApollo11
Okay. I'm about to head on back up the ladder and into Eagle unless Houston has anything more for me.

Bruce McCandless @BMCAPCOM
Nothing more for Buzz. He can head on up the ladder at this time.

Walter Cronkite @WCCBSNews
As the astronauts prepare to climb back into Eagle and leave the Moon, because of weight concerns they will be leaving behind many thousands of dollars-worth of equipment to remain un-used on the lunar surface. NASA has been criticized for this.

Walter Cronkite @WCCBSNews
However, one of the officials in Houston remarked a while back that, "We know what an $11,000 camera looks like. We don't know what moon rocks look like."

Walter Cronkite @WCCBSNews
Buzz Aldrin is now climbing up the ladder and back into lunar module Eagle. No problem getting up those steps in one-sixth gravity.

Buzz Aldrin @LMPApollo11
I'm getting back aboard Eagle and getting the lunar equipment conveyer all ready to bring up the rock box.

Walter Cronkite @WCCBSNews
Buzz Aldrin has now completed his walk on the Moon. He's back onboard Eagle and soon to be joined by Mission Commander Neil Armstrong.

Bruce McCandless @BMCAPCOM
Neil has confirmed that the Hasselblad camera magazine is now going up into Eagle attached to the sample return container.

Wally Schirra @WSNASA
The astronauts are working with the 'clothes line', transferring the sample containers up into the lunar module.

Neil Armstrong @CMDRApollo11
Uh-oh! The film pack just came off the sample return container.

Buzz Aldrin @LMPApollo11
We just need to ease the lunar equipment conveyer back down, gently, not pulling too hard and re-attach the camera magazine to the sample return container.

Neil Armstrong @CMDRApollo11
Okay. I've got one side hooked up to the second box. The film pack is now firmly attached and I'm sending it up.

Buzz Aldrin @LMPApollo11
If Neil can just kind of hold it, I think I can do the pulling.

Bruce McCandless @BMCAPCOM
Neil has now been on the lunar surface just a little bit longer than two hours. The observatory in California reports a return on the laser experiment. Looks like Neil and Buzz set it up just perfectly.

Walter Cronkite @WCCBSNews
So the laser reflector experiment is already up and running. Quite incredible just how well everything in this mission has gone so far.

Walter Cronkite @WCCBSNews
These two astronauts have had a very long day. They've been up now for 18 hours and 10 minutes with no rest break in between.

Buzz Aldrin @LMPApollo11
Okay. The package is up and unhooked. We have the Hasselblad magazine and a large selection of carefully selected, if not documented, rock samples now onboard Eagle.

Neil Armstrong @CMDRApollo11
We ran out of time on collecting documented samples but I think we got enough really good stuff to keep the boffins back on Earth busy for years to come. I'm heading up the ladder now to join Buzz.

Wally Schirra @WSNASA
Okay. Armstrong is now climbing the ladder and getting aboard lunar module Eagle once more. One more step and there he goes.

Buzz Aldrin @LMPApollo11
We're both back inside Eagle now, maneuvering slowly around each other to get straight... not easy. I'll get the hatch.

Buzz Aldrin @LMPApollo11
Okay. The hatch is now closed, latched and verified secure.

Jules Bergman @JBABCNews
Both astronauts are once again inside lunar module Eagle having successfully completed their walk on the surface of the Moon.

Jules Bergman @JBABCNews
About an hour and ten minutes from now, they will re-open the hatch door and throw out all the unnecessary items they don't need to bring back and leave them on the surface of the Moon.

Neil Armstrong @CMDRApollo11
We have feedwater valves set to CLOSED.

Bruce McCandless @BMCAPCOM
Neil is cutting out. He's not readable.

Bruce McCandless @BMCAPCOM
We're not reading Buzz either... nothing but static. Standing by.

Bruce McCandless @BMCAPCOM
I just copied a transmission calling Houston. All else was broken up. We are reading neither of the astronauts at this time.

Bruce McCandless @BMCAPCOM
If they can hear us inside Eagle, we're asking them to un-stow one portable life system antenna so we can have communications.

Bruce McCandless @BMCAPCOM
Still not able to establish contact with the astronauts aboard lunar module Eagle.

Buzz Aldrin @LMPApollo11
Looking around the inside of the LEM I can see something that shouldn't be here – a broken off part of a circuit breaker.

Neil Armstrong @CMDRApollo11
We've had a potentially serious mishap here. While getting settled back in Eagle, Buzz spun around and his bulky portable life support system banged into the circuit breaker panel.

Buzz Aldrin @LMPApollo11
Of all the circuit breakers that could have been damaged, it had to be the one that controls the ascent engine. Part of the small control switch broke off and settled onto the floor of the LEM.

Neil Armstrong @CMDRApollo11
The remaining part of the circuit breaker will probably hold, but we have to make sure that the circuit breaker doesn't automatically disengage the ascent engine as we lift off. That would be catastrophic.

Neil Armstrong @CMDRApollo11
To improve our chances of getting a successful ascent engine burn we are taking a plastic pen, breaking off a piece and jamming it in to hold the circuit breaker in place.

Buzz Aldrin @LMPApollo11
That's one hell of a high technology fix we just improvised there. If it works, it could become a recommended NASA procedure for future missions in such a circumstance.

Jules Bergman @JBABCNews
The difficulty with communications at this point is only with voice transmission, not with telemetry. NASA continues to receive good telemetry from lunar module Eagle down to Houston.

Neil Armstrong @CMDRApollo11
Okay. We're back in communication with Houston. That was a nervy few minutes. We're now in the process of switching over to lunar module comms.

Jules Bergman @JBABCNews
The lunar module is now being re-pressurized, and the telemetry Mission Control is receiving clearly indicates that.

Dr. Thomas Gold @TGCornell
Now that the lunar module is being pressurized and oxygen introduced to the cabin once more, comes I

believe, one of the most unknown and potentially disastrous aspects of this mission.

Dr. Thomas Gold @TGCornell
The rocks and soil samples the astronauts have brought into the lunar module have never been exposed to oxygen or to a pressurized environment.

Dr. Thomas Gold @TGCornell
Many of us believe those samples will be pyrophoric – that is: capable of igniting spontaneously when exposed to air. They may well smolder and burst into flames as the cabin re-pressurizes and oxygen is re-introduced.

Buzz Aldrin @LMPApollo11
We are well aware of the geologists' concerns regarding the rock and soil samples and so we are conducting an ad hoc moon dust test. Neil is unpacking his initial small 'grab sample'.

Neil Armstrong @CMDRApollo11
The grab specimen was only taken in case we had to make an immediate emergency evacuation from the surface. Since we didn't, and have lots of other samples, we can afford to conduct this little experiment just to be on the safe side.

Buzz Aldrin @LMPApollo11
We are placing the grab sample on the cylindrical flat top of the Eagle's ascent engine. We will be sure to keep a close eye on it as the cabin re-pressurizes and oxygen is re-introduced.

Buzz Aldrin @LMPApollo11
If the sample starts to smoke and smolder, we will stop cabin pressurization, open the hatch and toss the sample out.

Michael Collins @CMPApollo11
I have just heard from Houston that the crew of Tranquility Base is back inside Eagle and that everything on the surface went beautifully... Hallelujah!

Walter Cronkite @WCCBSNews
We now have just one more critical function of the mission as far as the Moon landing part of the mission is concerned – lift off of the lunar module from the lunar surface.

Walter Cronkite @WCCBSNews
Well, then there's then also the 'critical' docking with the command module. Then the 'critical' firing of the main engine to get the spaceship in a trajectory to get them on their way back to Earth.

Wally Schirra @WSNASA
Then there's the 'critical' separation from the service module, the 'critical' re-entry, the 'critical' opening of the parachutes and the 'critical' recovery.

Walter Cronkite @WCCBSNews
So, still many critical stages yet to come and we hardly have the right to be blasé about what is an extremely dangerous business, in which the failure of any one stage could result in the loss of the entire mission and the lives of three brave astronauts.

Walter Cronkite @WCCBSNews
Nobody likes to think of such a circumstance, but the unspoken fear of many is that the Eagle may fail to lift off from the lunar surface. Since such a lift off has never been tried before, there are many unknowns.

Walter Cronkite @WCCBSNews
We understand that should such a disastrous scenario unfold, there will be no second chances and no rescue plan. The astronauts would remain on the Moon to pass away through slow starvation or "deliberately closed down communications."

Walter Cronkite @WCCBSNews
Nobody at NASA has been forthcoming as to what "closed down communications" means or implies, but I think many of us can guess.

Wally Schirra @WSNASA
We were asked, early on in the program, what is the most dangerous part of the mission. The answer was: "the part between the countdown to lift off and recovery after landing back on Earth." I think that still applies.

Bruce McCandless @BMCAPCOM
We've completed the uplink and handed back the computer to Mike Collins on Columbia and asked him to do another optics update to see if he can locate the lunar module on this pass.

Buzz Aldrin @LMPApollo11
Still keeping the occasional eye on the grab sample. No sign yet of the material igniting. Looks like we have a GO to bring the rock and soil samples back to Earth.

Neil Armstrong @CMDRApollo11
We're now using up what LEM film we have left and about to change the primary environmental control system canister. Just snapped a photo of the stars and stripes as seen from Eagle.

Neil Armstrong @CMDRApollo11
I'm wondering how much longer we want to wait. We've probably got another half hour of picture-taking. I guess we could go through an eat cycle, and then change the CO_2 canister before preparing for lift off.

Neil Armstrong @CMDRApollo11
Houston agreed to my suggested cycle. Guess it'll continue being a little crowded in here for a while.

Michael Collins @CMPApollo11
I now have the revised coordinates Houston sent up to help me try to locate lunar module Eagle on the Moon's surface. Trying to locate the lunar module now.

Michael Collins @CMPApollo11
Nope. Can't see them.

Bruce McCandless @BMCAPCOM
Mike might be interested in knowing that we now have gotten reflections back from the laser reflector Neil and Buzz set up. We may be able to get more accurate location information from that in a short while.

Michael Collins @CMPApollo11
I do need very a very precise position because I can only do a decent job of scanning maybe one of those grid squares at a time.

Bruce McCandless @BMCAPCOM
We appreciate Mike's issue and intend this to be the last optics update we'll have him do aboard the command ship. We don't want to use up too much fuel in this effort.

Michael Collins @CMPApollo11
There's currently no problem fuel wise. It's just that there is a limit to the number of optics updates and the number of grid squares I can search over to find Eagle.

Walter Cronkite @WCCBSNews
The time of the extra vehicular activity has now been officially recorded as 2 hours and 31 minutes, as

against the time in the flight plan timeline of 2 hours and 40 minutes.

Walter Cronkite @WCCBSNews
We are told that President Nixon joked that he hoped he would not be billed for his call to the astronauts on the Moon.

Wally Schirra @WSNASA
A telephone call over a distance of 250,000 miles could come in a little expensive for the White House, although I'm not even sure if there is an area code for the Moon.

Walter Cronkite @WCCBSNews
We haven't heard any communication from the astronauts on the lunar surface for quite some time now which is a little worrying.

Walter Cronkite @WCCBSNews
With Mike Collins in the command ship about to go around the far side of the Moon, he will no longer be able to relay the signal which he had done previously.

Walter Cronkite @WCCBSNews
I am assured that despite lack of voice comms, telemetry coming down from the lunar module, including telemetry from the bio-sensors the astronauts are wearing, indicates that all remains well up there on the Moon.

Bruce McCandless @BMCAPCOM
Command ship Columbia is now a little less than 2 minutes to loss of signal. Next acquisition of signal will be at 114 hours 04 minutes mission time.

Bruce McCandless @BMCAPCOM
If it's agreeable with Mike, we'd like him to stay awake until we have one more re-acquisition on the high gain antenna. He can plan on turning in after the acquisition of signal on the next pass.

4 days 17 hours 16 minutes mission time

Bruce McCandless @BMCAPCOM
My team and I will be taking a day off tomorrow. What a great day today was. I really enjoyed it. Maybe the best day ever.

Neil Armstrong @CMDRApollo11
Glad Bruce enjoyed guiding us through today's activities on the lunar surface. I think Buzz and I may have enjoyed it even more than Bruce and his team.

Neil Armstrong @CMDRApollo11
You can't really count on things going as smoothly as they did today with no major hiccups, apart from being behind the optimal timeline at some points.

Bruce McCandless @BMCAPCOM
I just told Neil I sure wish he's hurry up getting that trash out of there. Also, suit relief valve is still in the AUTO position. It should be closed.

Bruce McCandless @BMCAPCOM
We have successfully re-acquired the high-gain antenna signal with Mike and Columbia. Unless he has any more traffic with us, we will bid him goodnight and let him get some sleep.

Michael Collins @CMPApollo11
I'm turning in for the night, hoping to wake up fresh and alert to welcome Neil and Buzz back to the

mother ship after their successful excursion on the surface of the Moon.

Bruce McCandless @BMCAPCOM
We will power down the voice subcarrier part of our uplink to Mike in Columbia so that we don't disturb him while we are talking to Tranquility Base.

Michael Collins @CMPApollo11
If Mike needs us, he can give us a call and we will respond with a time lag of about a minute to a minute and a half in that configuration.

Neil Armstrong @CMDRApollo11
We've used the forward dump valve until about 2 psi. We're using the overhead dump valve now. They're both open at the moment.

Bruce McCandless @BMCAPCOM
Tranquility Base now reports. "DEPRESS complete".

Bruce McCandless @BMCAPCOM
We observed Eagle's equipment jettison on the TV, and the passive seismic experiment they set up recorded shocks as each piece of discarded equipment hit the lunar surface. That's amazing!

Neil Armstrong @CMDRApollo11
Houston saw us, and the seismometer recorded us littering the Moon? Wow! You can't get away with anything anymore, can you?

Bruce McCandless @BMCAPCOM
When Neil and Buzz are ready to turn in shortly, we'd like them to go back to caution and warning ENABLE.

Bruce McCandless @BMCAPCOM
And we'd like to say from all of us down here in
Houston, and really from all the countries in the entire
world, we think they did a truly magnificent job up
there today.

Buzz Aldrin @LMPApollo11
We thanked Houston for the very kind words. Today
has been a long day. We need to get some rest now
and have at it tomorrow.

Bruce McCandless @BMCAPCOM
We have a set of questions relating to things Neil and
Buzz observed during the EVA. They can discuss them
a little later this evening or sometime later in the
mission. Up to them.

Buzz Aldrin @LMPApollo11
I guess we can take some questions at this point and
put off our sleep period for a while.

Bruce McCandless @BMCAPCOM
My friendly Green Team here in Houston is now being
relieved by Owen and his also-friendly Maroon Team.
Owen will relay the questions up to the Eagle crew.

Owen Garriott @OGCAPCOM
Several of the questions relate to the depth and
surface characteristics in the areas where the bulk
samples were collected. Neil is giving detailed
technical responses to the questions.

Neil Armstrong @CMDRApollo11
In response to the question about the time limitation,
I explained that I had half of the larger sample bag
full of assorted rocks that I hurriedly picked up from

around the area. I tried to get as many representative samples as I could.

Owen Garriott @OGCAPCOM
A lot of very technical, geological questions we're putting to the crew now. Not sure they are really qualified to answer, but they're doing a pretty fine job of it anyway.

Owen Garriott @OGCAPCOM
The NASA geologists here are asking if the crew has any more lengthy description or detailed description of the general geology of the area.

Buzz Aldrin @LMPApollo11
We have a great deal we could say about the general geology of the area, but I think we can leave that until later.

Owen Garriott @OGCAPCOM
I think that's enough of the questions from our geologists tonight. Unless the crew of Eagle have any more for us, that will be all from us for the evening.

NO CONTACT FOR 6 HOURS 6 MINUTES

Ronald Evans @RECAPCOM
I'm back in the chair with my Black Team. About to wake up Tranquility Base and Columbia.

Ronald Evans @RECAPCOM
We have re-established contact with Mike in the command ship after what we hope was a good night's sleep and we're about to have him do a guidance platform realignment.

Michael Collins @CMPApollo11
I think I got about 5 hours of good sleep, although the guys back in Houston probably have a better readout on that than I do due to these biomed sensors stuck to my body.

Ronald Evans @RECAPCOM
We have a lot more detail for Mike's next optics update which we are sending up to him now. This will properly position his rendezvous radar transponder.

Michael Collins @CMPApollo11
Houston also needs to send me the grid square of crater 130.

Ronald Evans @RECAPCOM
We're working on the grid squares and will get them up to Mike in Columbia shortly.

Michael Collins @CMPApollo11
Houston have updated their tracking information and I now have their best estimate as to where exactly lunar module Eagle is right now.

Ronald Evans @RECAPCOM
We don't think our best estimate of Eagle's position is necessarily terribly accurate. When they carry out their optics update on Mike's transponder, that will be our last shot at fixing Eagle's location.

Neil Armstrong @CMDRApollo11
Houston just got back in touch and Ron Evans asked me about our sleep period and if I managed to get a chance to curl up on the engine can.

Buzz Aldrin @LMPApollo11
For our sleep period inside lunar module Eagle, Neil managed to rig himself a really good hammock with a waste tether and he's been lying on the ascent engine cover. I curled up on the floor.

Buzz Aldrin @LMPApollo11
Houston wants us to do an optics update tracking command module Columbia for one last shot at getting a fix on our position on the lunar surface.

5 days 1 hour 42 minutes mission time

Ronald Evans @RECAPCOM
Eagle is now carrying out one last vent of the descent propulsion system. We are now reading up to Neil the procedures and settings he needs to institute at TIG (time of ignition) minus 17 minutes.

Ronald Evans @RECAPCOM
Meanwhile, Mike in Columbia needs to stir up all four of his CRYO tanks for the standard one minute.

Buzz Aldrin @LMPApollo11
The lunar module guidance computer self test is now complete and Houston tells me it is a GO.

Michael Collins @CMPApollo11
CRYO stir is now complete. No issues there, and my rendezvous radar tracking is now operating.

Ronald Evans @RECAPCOM
Tranquility base should now go ahead and start warming up on the rendezvous radar.

Ronald Evans @RECAPCOM
Command ship Columbia will be directly overhead
Eagle at Tranquility Base at 122 hours 22 minutes 51
seconds elapsed mission time—six minutes from now.

Buzz Aldrin @LMPApollo11
We expect that we may lose lock with Columbia as it
passes overhead because of the maximum range that
the radar has.

Neil Armstrong @CMDRApollo11
We just lost radar lock.

Buzz Aldrin @LMPApollo11
Houston needs to tell us if Mike has already gone
overhead, or if they want us to try to establish lock on
again.

Ronald Evans @RECAPCOM
Buzz should try to get back in radar lock. If he can,
he'll still lose Columbia again in 29 minutes and 35
seconds.

Ronald Evans @RECAPCOM
We are now recommending Tranquility Base terminate
their optics update. From what we are seeing down
here, radar thinks the range is greater than 400 miles
now.

Ronald Evans @RECAPCOM
Getting an awful lot of static on the comms now. We
have to ask the crew to repeat their updates over and
over. It's very frustrating.

Neil Armstrong @CMDRApollo11
We have four out of eight circuit breakers indicating red right now. I need Houston to tell me if it is normal to have these four red flags.

Ronald Evans @RECAPCOM
We believe the circuit breakers condition is normal at this time. Neil can go ahead and reset them and press ahead towards hot fire.

Neil Armstrong @CMDRApollo11
Stargazing now. I used Capella in the last sighting, but I'm wondering if it would pay to use Alpheratz star number 1. It might be a little closer. However, it would delay things a little since I'd have to designate the radar out of the way.

Ronald Evans @RECAPCOM
We would prefer to save the time and press on with Capella. We now have the full range of lunar module ascent coordinates which we are currently sending up to Tranquility Base.

Ronald Evans @RECAPCOM
Lunar module ascent lift off time is now scheduled for exactly 124 hours 22 minutes elapsed mission time. Less than one and a half hours from now.

Ronald Evans @RECAPCOM
We have Columbia's consumables update ready to read up to Mike. Hydrogen total is minus 1.4 pounds. Oxygen is plus 1.7.

Michael Collins @CMPApollo11
Whoever figured out those oxygens and hydrogens a couple of days ago must have known what he was

doing. Less than two minutes now to next loss of signal as I make another lonely turn around the Moon.

Jim Lovell @JLNASA
On behalf of myself and the backup crew, I just sent up our congratulations to Columbia and Eagle for yesterday's excellent performance and sent up our prayers for a successful lift off and rendezvous.

Michael Collins @CMPApollo11
We're glad to have a big room down there in Houston full of people looking over our shoulder.

Neil Armstrong @CMDRApollo11
I told Jimbo we had a great deal of help getting down here and handling the lunar excursion effectively. This has been far from a 3-man mission. It has a cast of thousands.

Ronald Evans @RECAPCOM
Eagle is looking real fine to us down here. We have fairly high confidence that we now know the position of the lunar module. However, it is possible that we may have a planes change, but at worst it will be 30 feet per second.

Michael Collins @CMPApollo11
Back in contact with Houston now. Ron tells me their updated position for Tranquility Base is just west of the crater Juliet.

Buzz Aldrin @LMPApollo11
Because of the lower load with the rendezvous radar off, we're putting batteries 5 and 6 online now. Batteries 1 and 3 off.

Michael Collins @CMPApollo11
I am holding Columbia inertially at lift off attitude. Digital autopilot is configured according to the previously determined procedures.

Ronald Evans @RECAPCOM
About to give Columbia a mark at 20 minutes to GO.

Ronald Evans @RECAPCOM
Mark! ... Our guidance recommendation is primary guidance and navigation system on the lunar module is good. Lunar module Eagle is cleared for lift off.

Neil Armstrong @CMDRApollo11
We are not sure we can get tank number 2 firing at this time. It's still showing a high pressure.

Buzz Aldrin @LMPApollo11
I don't think the pressure on tank number 2 is indicative of anything. I assume we are still GO for lift off at this point and am proceeding with the ascent feed.

Ronald Evans @RECAPCOM
We'll watch tank number 2. If the pressure doesn't decrease, we'll tell them to close the ascent feeds and open the shutoffs.

Michael Collins @CMPApollo11
I'm reading Neil on VHF now. Sounds really good. Less than 10 minutes to lift off of lunar module Eagle.

Neil Armstrong @CMDRApollo11
Things couldn't be going better now. It's just purring along.

Buzz Aldrin @LMPApollo11
We're standing by for 2 minutes for the guidance steering in the abort guidance system.

Buzz Aldrin @LMPApollo11
We now have guidance steering in the abort guidance system.

Ronald Evans @RECAPCOM
Two minutes to IGNITION of Eagle's lift off engine.

Dr. David Baker @DBNASA
This is such a critical moment. There is only one ascent engine on the LEM and it has to work. No second chances. That engine has never been tested.

Walter Cronkite @WCCBSNews
Never been tested? How can that be?

Dr. David Baker @DBNASA
I mean that particular engine has never been tested. The design has been tested, even on previous flights including on Apollo 10, but firing the engine and then reusing it is impossible.

Walter Cronkite @WCCBSNews
Why is that?

Dr. David Baker @DBNASA
Because of the massive corrosive effect of the particular propellant used to fire the engine, one successful firing renders the engine virtually destroyed.

Walter Cronkite @WCCBSNews
So that particular engine is new and untested. Wow! This really is a one shot thing.

Dr. David Baker @DBNASA
Yes. And of course, we've never attempted a lift off
from the Moon's surface before.

Walter Cronkite @WCCBSNews
Oh, boy! This is real nail-biting, white-knuckle stuff --
praying that that single engine will be good enough to
fire and lift those boys off the lunar surface.

William Safire @WSWhiteHouse
Haldeman has approved my final draft of the
president's speech to the nation in the event the
astronauts are unable to lift off from the Moon. I am
only posting the contents to my close circle.

William Safire @WSWhiteHouse
If the speech is not needed, its contents will be kept
confidential for decades. It begins: "Fate has ordained
that the men who went to the Moon will stay on the
Moon to rest in peace."

William Safire @WSWhiteHouse
It continues: "These brave men know that there is no
hope for their recovery. But they also know that there
is hope for mankind in their sacrifice."

William Safire @WSWhiteHouse
"These two men are laying down their lives in
mankind's most noble goal: the search for truth and
understanding."

William Safire @WSWhiteHouse
"They will be mourned by their families and friends;
they will be mourned by their nation; they will be
mourned by the people of the Earth and by a Mother

Earth that dared to send two of her sons into the unknown."

William Safire @WSWhiteHouse
"Others will follow and surely find their way home. Man's search will not be denied. But these men were the first and they will remain the foremost in our hearts."

William Safire @WSWhiteHouse
"For every human being that looks up at the Moon in the nights to come will know that there is some corner of another world that is forever mankind."

Walter Cronkite @WCCBSNews
We are now waiting on what could be the most critical stage of this entire mission — lift off from the lunar surface. Tension could not be higher at this point.

Ronald Evans @RECAPCOM
One minute to lift off...

Ronald Evans @RECAPCOM
Thirty seconds...

Buzz Aldrin @LMPApollo11
Master arm ON. 9... 8... 7... 6... 5... engine arm ascent!

Buzz Aldrin @LMPApollo11
3.. 2..1.. Lift off!

Buzz Aldrin @LMPApollo11
Beautiful!

Buzz Aldrin @LMPApollo11
26... 36 feet per second up... Pitchover... Very smooth... Balance couple OFF... Very quiet ride so far.

Ronald Evans @RECAPCOM
Eagle remains GO at 1 minute and looking good.
We're requesting manual start override at this time.

Buzz Aldrin @LMPApollo11
It's a very quiet ride. Just a little bit of slow wallowing
back and forth. Not much thruster activity.

Ronald Evans @RECAPCOM
Eagle remains GO at 3 minutes. Everything continues
to look good.

Ronald Evans @RECAPCOM
Four minutes and Eagle is right down the track.
Everything is looking great!

Buzz Aldrin @LMPApollo11
We have the crater Sabine off to our right now and I
can also see craters Ritter and Schmidt. Really
impressive looking.

Neil Armstrong @CMDRApollo11
This is one pretty spectacular ride!

Michael Collins @CMPApollo11
I have a solid lock on the VHF ranging of Eagle — 480
feet per second.

Neil Armstrong @CMDRApollo11
480 feet per second sounds a little high, but no
problem.

Michael Collins @CMPApollo11
Eagle can now go ahead with the guidance platform
realignment as scheduled.

Neil Armstrong @CMDRApollo11
The Eagle is now back in orbit, having left Tranquility Base and leaving behind on the lunar surface a replica of our Apollo 11 patch with an eagle and olive branch.

Walter Cronkite @WCCBSNews
I guess Armstrong deliberately omitted that they also left behind the Stars and Stripes. Good idea. The whole world, not just the U.S., is immensely proud of what those guys have accomplished.

Ronald Evans @RECAPCOM
We are giving Columbia a good GO lunar module vector. After he goes to ACCEPT, we will hand him back the computer.

Buzz Aldrin @LMPApollo11
I am maneuvering Eagle toward rendezvous coordinates for our docking with Columbia.

Ronald Evans @RECAPCOM
We are seeing a jump in cabin and suit pressure on Eagle. They need to verify the REPRESS valve is closed.

Neil Armstrong @CMDRApollo11
REPRESS valve is closed and has been for some time.

Ronald Evans @RECAPCOM
We are losing data from Eagle, but they have about one minute before they ought to be able to track Columbia by radar.

Michael Collins @CMPApollo11
The VHF ranging is not working.

Buzz Aldrin @LMPApollo11

Houston has confirmed that they copy our star angle difference and torquing angles.

Ronald Evans @RECAPCOM
We didn't get the star angle difference on the downlink but on the VOX. Eagle now needs to go to pitch 162, yaw minus 16.

Michael Collins @CMPApollo11
I am unable to read Eagle on either antenna or on VHF. I have asked Houston if they have any suggestions.

Neil Armstrong @CMDRApollo11
We are reading Columbia, but very weakly.

Michael Collins @CMPApollo11
Also, my VHF ranging is not working. I need to know if Houston would like me to continue making sextant marks or do nothing. I'm supposed to be doing only VHF marks at this point.

Ronald Evans @RECAPCOM
We are working on Columbia's VHF issues. At this point, the best antenna position for lunar module Eagle should be forward. We recommend Columbia takes sextant marks at this time.

Michael Collins @CMPApollo11
Okay. I have the VHF ranging back now. I'll stick with the scheduled procedures from this point forward... hopefully.

Ronald Evans @RECAPCOM
That's good news from Columbia. Mike can go ahead and get as many VHF and sextant marks as he can in the next few minutes.

Michael Collins @CMPApollo11
I've just got time for maybe two sextant marks before getting on with the final count.

Ronald Evans @RECAPCOM
We now have about 1 minute before loss of signal from Columbia.

Buzz Aldrin @LMPApollo11
We are now GO for CSI (co-elliptic sequence initiation).

Ronald Evans @RECAPCOM
We are recommending that Eagle use aft OMNI comms when they go for CSI so that Mike on Columbia can know it has taken place successfully.

Michael Collins @CMPApollo11
I did not copy Eagle's GO or initiation for CSI. I am only reading them intermittingly.

Ronald Evans @RECAPCOM
Columbia is coming in very weak. We need Mike to continually repeat what he is saying.

Ronald Evans @RECAPCOM
Getting almost no communication from Columbia now. Really bad comms signal.

Buzz Aldrin @LMPApollo11
I think we can see Columbia coming up over the horizon. It looks like there is a laser operating. Asking Houston for confirmation.

Neil Armstrong @CMDRApollo11
Mike on Columbia has been reading Houston loud and clear, but he hasn't had any luck in transmitting to Houston.

Ronald Evans @RECAPCOM
We continue to hear Eagle perfectly, but nothing from Columbia.

Neil Armstrong @CMDRApollo11
We have an environmental control system warning light. A CO_2 light.

Ronald Evans @RECAPCOM
We're pretty sure the warning light is just a sensor problem. More worrying right now is our inability to read anything coming down from Mike Collins in Columbia.

Neil Armstrong @CMDRApollo11
And our water separator isn't working properly. We've changed water separators, but it doesn't seem to have improved the situation.

Ronald Evans @RECAPCOM
We need to know if Neil and Buzz have their liquid cooled suits hooked up properly and if so, what the suit accumulator indicates.

Buzz Aldrin @LMPApollo11
Our suits are hooked up fine. The water accumulator is now right on the line between the red and the green.

Ronald Evans @RECAPCOM
On the water problem, we can't add anything to it, except to say that the water accumulators look like they are up to speed to us down here.

Neil Armstrong @CMDRApollo11
The water problem is just in one suit for some reason. It's okay. It's not going to be too much of a problem.

Michael Collins @CMPApollo11
I'm passing over the landing site right now. It sure is great to look down there and not worry about seeing them on the surface anymore.

Michael Collins @CMPApollo11
I'm still not able to get Houston to read me from Columbia. All communication between us has to be relayed through the lunar module - a vehicle that we will be jettisoning shortly after docking and crew transfer into Columbia.

Ronald Evans @RECAPCOM
Our communications problem with command ship Columbia has now been traced to a ground station here. We expect it to be fixed shortly.

Michael Collins @CMPApollo11
The last TIG (time of ignition) I got was about 30 seconds earlier than mine. I need a new update from Eagle.

Buzz Aldrin @LMPApollo11
Our latest estimate for TIG is 127 hours 03 minutes 39 seconds elapsed mission time - in about 15 minutes.

Ronald Evans @RECAPCOM
Due to the possibility of water channeling inside Eagle, we are recommending the crew stay in CABIN mode. Helmets and gloves ON or OFF is up to them. We really have no concern with the CO_2.

Michael Collins @CMPApollo11
Houston (or somebody somewhere down the line) seems to have fixed the comms problem. We're reading each other real fine now.

Michael Collins @CMPApollo11
I am starting to maneuver to final phase initiation in preparation to receive lunar module Eagle and its returning crew.

Neil Armstrong @CMDRApollo11
Coming up on 1 minute to time of ignition. Everything is looking good.

Neil Armstrong @CMDRApollo11
We're burning...

Neil Armstrong @CMDRApollo11
Still burning...

Neil Armstrong @CMDRApollo11
Burn complete. No problems.

Neil Armstrong @CMDRApollo11
Real close to Columbia now. Trying to get in position for docking.

Lunar module Eagle approaching command module Columbia for docking

Neil Armstrong @CMDRApollo11
I can stop rolling right here if Mike likes this attitude. Then I'll just let her hold in ATTITUDE HOLD.

Michael Collins @CMPApollo11
Eagle is coming in slowly. Preparing to dock.

Michael Collins @CMPApollo11
Initiating docking.

Michael Collins @CMPApollo11
Okay. That's it! Successful docking with lunar module Eagle. That was a funny one — I didn't feel it shock when we connected.

Michael Collins @CMPApollo11
Okay. I have thrusters B3 and B4 safetied and am pumping up cabin pressure. Going through the post-docking checklist now.

Jules Bergman @JBABCNews
I am weakened to think just what has been accomplished here. NASA and the Apollo 11 crew have now performed flawlessly and overcome 8 of the 10 major engineering hurdles of the mission, those being the major rocket engine burns.

Jules Bergman @JBABCNews
Those engine burns were: the launch of the Saturn V rocket from Pad 39, the trans-lunar insertion burn a couple of hours later, the lunar orbit insertion burn almost 76 hours after lift off.

Jules Bergman @JBABCNews
Then, the descent orbit insertion burn, and the powered descent burn to the surface of the Moon.

Jules Bergman @JBABCNews
Then, that heart-stopping ascent engine burn that went so beautifully to lift them off the surface of the Moon, and the burn that but them into an orbit for rendezvous and the docking that the crew accomplished just minutes ago.

Jules Bergman @JBABCNews
An incredible rate of success – every burn has performed flawlessly so far.

Ronald Evans @RECAPCOM
Mike has now completed the tunnel leak check and is proceeding with opening the hatch dump valve.

Michael Collins @CMPApollo11
My hatch is now removed. Buzz can open his now.
Ron says Houston is reading us real well on the high
gain antenna now.

Jules Bergman @JBABCNews
The two major events that lie ahead for the crew are
the trans-Earth insertion burn later tonight or
tomorrow morning, depending on what Commander
Armstrong decides to do, and the re-entry and
splashdown on Thursday.

Jules Bergman @JBABCNews
Technology has triumphed here, and all I can think is
that the great genius of America is to take something
momentous and make it seem un-momentous. Only in
this case, it doesn't seem un-momentous to me.

Buzz Aldrin @LMPApollo11
Given all the comms problems we've been having,
Houston might want to give some thought to what will
happen to our comms when we jettison the lunar
module which has been the better vehicle as far as
comms is concerned.

Ronald Evans @RECAPCOM
Apollo 11 now also have their steerable antenna
angles for lunar module jettison, so there should be
few problems with comms from now on.

Michael Collins @CMPApollo11
Houston is sending up the roll, pitch and yaw attitudes
for jettisoning Eagle. I have them noted down.

Ronald Evans @RECAPCOM
Five minutes now to loss of signal as both command
module Columbia and attached lunar module Eagle

pass behind the Moon. Jettisoning of the lunar module will be at 131 hours 52 minutes elapsed mission time.

Ronald Evans @RECAPCOM
About a minute and a half to loss of signal. They are looking great. It's been a mighty fine day!

Michael Collins @CMPApollo11
Ron is not kidding there. It really has been "a mighty fine day."

Walter Cronkite @WCCBSNews
For a while today, Russia's Luna-15 caused a stir by landing on the Moon. But Moscow says that its work is "finished". Indications from Britain's Jodrell Bank radio telescope are that it landed hard and tonight lies damaged and silent on the lunar surface.

Tom Brokaw @TBNBCNews
As Americans tonight wait only for the safe return of the Apollo astronauts, many, many other Americans here on Earth also face danger in a remote country halfway across the globe called Vietnam.

Tom Brokaw @TBNBCNews
Today was no national holiday to watch the Moon landing for many of these young men serving in our armed forces in Vietnam.

Tom Brokaw @TBNBCNews
I spoke today with several tired and dirty American GIs who had just returned from a night patrol that had been ambushed by the Viet Cong to learn that two of their countrymen had landed on the Moon.

Tom Brokaw @TBNBCNews
But what was more important to those GIs was the knowledge that they had survived another night on Earth.

PVT. Pete Harrris @PHDaNang
We heard a bit about it before the landing, but we were pretty busy while they were landing. Glad they made it though. Glad me and my buddies made it through today too.

SGT. Bill Mortlock @BMDa Nang
Proud of those guys up there on the Moon. Even prouder of the platoon leader who brought those guys out of that VC ambush with only light casualties. It could have been much much worse.

Walter Cronkite @WCCBSNews
At the Vatican's splendidly-equipped observatory near his summer residence at Castel Gandolfo southeast of Rome, Pope Paul followed the events of the unbelievable night.

Walter Cronkite @WCCBSNews
Like thousands of others throughout Italy waiting for word of a successful landing, the Pope leaned forward toward the TV and applauded enthusiastically when the announcer exclaimed (in Italian of course) that Eagle had touched down on the Moon.

Walter Cronkite @WCCBSNews
Though an estimated 600 million people watched the Apollo landing, they are far outnumbered by the 800 million persons around the world who are totally unaware that men have landed on the Moon.

Walter Cronkite @WCCBSNews
Communist China, North Korea, North Vietnam and
Albania chose to keep their people in ignorance of the
accomplishment of Apollo 11.

Senator Ribicoff @ARUSSenate
I have informed my fellow senators that I intend to
introduce a bill in Congress to make July 20th. a
national holiday. My bill will propose the holiday be
called 'Apollo 11 Day'.

Eric Sevaroid @ESCBSNews
Every period of great human creativity has been
accompanied by, or immediately preceded by, much
mass violence. It means, apparently, that that is the
time when the human drive to come to a boil.

Eric Sevaroid @ESCBSNews
Then, you get wars, arson, riots in the streets and...
flights to the Moon.

Eric Sevaroid @ESCBSNews
Somebody else will have to decide if wars, riots and
manned space flights are better for the human spirit
than boredom.

Charlie Duke @CDCAPCOM
It looks like the crew are ahead of the timeline at this
point, so we'd like to move up jettisoning of Eagle to
130 hours 30 minutes if that's okay with the crew.

Michael Collins @CMPApollo11
Speeding up the timeline and jettisoning Eagle early is
fine with us, although I suspect Neil and Buzz will feel
pretty sad seeing their lunar module home-away-
from-home slowly drift off into oblivion.

5 days 10 hours 9 minutes mission time

Charlie Duke @CDCAPCOM
We're now thinking that moving up the jettison time would require a new attitude and we can't do that due to the lunar module being already closed out. It would fight us all the way around and we'd lose comms.

Neil Armstrong @CMDRApollo11
Mike has completed his checklist for jettisoning of lunar module Eagle and we are now waiting for a final GO from Houston.

Charlie Duke @CDCAPCOM
Columbia has a GO for jettison. They can undock now at their convenience.

Michael Collins @CMPApollo11
Okay. We will let go of Eagle in 10 seconds... Here goes...

Michael Collins @CMPApollo11
4... 3... 2... 1....Okay. A fairly loud noise and she appears to be departing, I guess at several feet per second.

Neil Armstrong @CMDRApollo11
There she goes indeed. She sure was a good ship.

Jules Bergman @JBABCNews
Lunar module Eagle will now orbit the Moon for several months until it eventually crashes into the lunar surface. Kind of sad.

Charlie Duke @CDCAPCOM
Mike doesn't need to try and chase the departing Eagle - only hold his current attitude.

Neil Armstrong @CMDRApollo11
It will take Apollo 11 a couple of minutes to integrate the detailed vectors we sent up for the next burn. If they don't make the scheduled timeline, it's no problem.

Michael Collins @CMPApollo11
Okay. We have everything vectored in. Preparing now to burn Columbia's engines.

Michael Collins @CMPApollo11
Burning.

Michael Collins @CMPApollo11
Burn complete.

Charlie Duke @CDCAPCOM
We copied Columbia's completed burn. Looked good to us down here.

Michael Collins @CMPApollo11
What we need now is a stable communications link between now and when we maneuver for trans-Earth attitude.

Charlie Duke @CDCAPCOM
Mike can now maneuver to his preliminary trans-Earth injection attitude as shown on page 398 of the flight plan. The high-gain antenna angles are good as shown in the flight plan.

Michael Collins @CMPApollo11
Now maneuvering and thankfully reading Houston loud and clear on the high-gain antenna.

Charlie Duke @CDCAPCOM
Nominal time for trans-Earth injection would be 135 hours 25 minutes elapsed mission time. However, we still need some more tracking so we can give Apollo 11 a good trans-Earth injection.

Charlie Duke @CDCAPCOM
Mike's little maneuver a while back will have Columbia put them about 20 miles ahead of lunar module Eagle by the time of trans-Earth injection.

Michael Collins @CMPApollo11
Charlie Duke just told me that Mission Control has now cleared out a bit after rendezvous and jettison. They all now have a place to sit. For me, it feels damn good to have some company up here once again.

Charlie Duke @CDCAPCOM
I asked Mike if he started talking to himself after all those turns around the Moon on his lonesome.

Michael Collins @CMPApollo11
I didn't really feel too lonesome. More like I had a couple of hundred million Americans up here with me—at least in spirit.

Charlie Duke @CDCAPCOM
Well, the American people could certainly see what they are getting for their money. And we heard that last night, after the landing, the New York Times printed the largest headline they have printed in their history.

Michael Collins @CMPApollo11
I've asked Charlie Duke to try and save me a copy of that New York Times front page.

Neil Armstrong @CMDRApollo11
Like Mike, I'm just glad to hear that the story and the headline were fit to print.

Charlie Duke @CDCAPCOM
That's why we didn't read up a newscast yesterday. There was really no other news worth talking about other than the successful Moon landing.

Charlie Duke @CDCAPCOM
We have ten minutes to next loss of signal. We'll have them coming back over the hill at 131 hours 48 minutes elapsed mission time.

5 days 12 hours 16 minutes mission time

Neil Armstrong @CMDRApollo11
Okay. We're back from behind the Moon and in touch with Houston once more. I believe they now have the latest newscast to read up to us.

Charlie Duke @CDCAPCOM
Congratulatory messages from world leaders on the Apollo 11 mission have been pouring into the White House in a steady stream all day, and the world's press has been dominated by news of the Apollo 11 mission.

Charlie Duke @CDCAPCOM
The New York Times will reprint today's edition on Thursday as a souvenir edition. Soviet Premier Alexei Kosygin has sent congratulations to the Apollo 11 crew and President Nixon through former Vice-President Humphrey who is currently visiting Russia.

Charlie Duke @CDCAPCOM
Mrs. Robert Goddard said that her husband would have been so happy to have witnessed the landing, but he wouldn't have shouted or jumped up and down. He would have just glowed. This was his dream - sending a manned rocket to the Moon.

Charlie Duke @CDCAPCOM
The Italian police reported that during the time of the Moon landing, they recorded their most crime-free period in recent history.

Charlie Duke @CDCAPCOM
In London a man who had the faith to place a small bet with a bookie that a man would reach the Moon before 1970 collected $24,000.

Neil Armstrong @CMDRApollo11
The guy won $24,000 for a small stake? Wow! Those must have been quite some odds. Good on him!

Charlie Duke @CDCAPCOM
In other exploration-related news, Thor Heyerdahl had to give up his attempt to sail a papyrus boat across the Atlantic. The storm-damaged boat was abandoned about 650 miles from Bermuda.

Neil Armstrong @CMDRApollo11
Charlie Duke also read up a whole lot of the latest sports news. Not worth noting here, except that the Astros have a record of 48 wins and 48 losses and are now in fifth place, seven games out.

Charlie Duke @CDCAPCOM
Seven minutes now to next loss of signal and Apollo 11 is looking good going over the hill once more.

5 days 13 hours 49 minutes mission time

Charlie Duke @CDCAPCOM
Back in touch with Apollo 11 as they come around the Moon, and we are asking the crew to stir up the CRYOs on this pass.

Michael Collins @CMPApollo11
The O_2 fuel cell purge is complete.

Charlie Duke @CDCAPCOM
We have a great deal of detailed coordinates and settings which we are currently sending up to Columbia relating to their coming home procedures. The burn to depart lunar orbit will be 2 ft/second as in the flight plan.

Charlie Duke @CDCAPCOM
Apollo 11 is now GO for trans-Earth injection burn.
Eight minutes to loss of signal. Burn will be at 135
hours 34 minutes 05 seconds elapsed mission time.

Neil Armstrong @CMDRApollo11
We are now back in touch with Houston after our final
trip around the back side of the Moon. The burn to
leave lunar orbit went beautifully - they don't make
them any finer, and we are now on a course heading
back to Earth.

Charlie Duke @CDCAPCOM
What a day this has been! Those guys are doing such
a fine job. I'm handing over my CAPCOM chair to Deke
Slayton now and heading off to get some well-earned
rest.

Deke Slayton @DSCAPCOM
Good to be back in the chair here at Mission Control.
Those guys really have been putting on a great show.
Now it's time for them to start powering down and get
a little rest - they've had a mighty long day.

Neil Armstrong @CMDRApollo11
Deke just told us that the guidance computer on our
jettisoned lunar module Eagle finally went belly up at
7 hours. Kind of sad... death of a real winner there!

6 days 3 hours mission time

Buzz Aldrin @LMPApollo11
Early morning update from Houston has us to do a
CO_2 filter change. At 148 hours, initiate a charge on
battery A instead of at 151 hours.

Buzz Aldrin @LMPApollo11
At 150 hours, we will do a wastewater dump to 10%, and we are told that we need to do the midcourse correction burn at 5 feet per second at about the nominal time in the flight plan.

Bruce McCandless @BMCAPCOM
We are seeing an erratic electrocardiograph reading for Buzz. He needs to check his biomedical sensors for a loose or dried out sensor.

Bruce McCandless @BMCAPCOM
We now have Apollo 11 as leaving the lunar sphere of influence and firmly on their way back home. If the crew are not too busy right now, we can read them the morning news from the home planet.

Neil Armstrong @CMDRApollo11
Ah, the news from Earth to be read up to us by Bruce. People back home may be surprised to learn that we really do look forward to, and appreciate, these regular news updates.

Bruce McCandless @BMCAPCOM
Apollo 11 still dominates the news around the world. Only 4 nations: Communist China, North Korea, North Vietnam and Albania, have not informed their citizens of the Moon landing.

Japanese family watching live coverage of the Apollo 11 mission

Bruce McCandless @BMCAPCOM
Tonight, President Nixon is scheduled to watch the All Star baseball game in Washington. After the game, he will depart for the Pacific recovery area.

Bruce McCandless @BMCAPCOM
On Thursday morning, the president will be aboard the USS Hornet in time to watch the splashdown of Apollo 11.

Bruce McCandless @BMCAPCOM
The Soviet spaceship Luna-15 is believed to have crashed into the Moon's Sea of Crisis after orbiting the Moon 52 times. The Soviet News Agency reported that "scientific research in near-Moon space has been carried out."

Bruce McCandless @BMCAPCOM
Things have been relatively quiet in Vietnam. Some GIs on patrol were reported to have been carrying transistor radios tuned to the flight of Apollo 11.

Skirmishes still continue between the Egyptians and Israelis along the Suez Canal.

Bruce McCandless @BMCAPCOM
Last night in New York, the Baseball Writers Association of America named Babe Ruth the greatest ball player of all time.

Bruce McCandless @BMCAPCOM
Joe DiMaggio was named greatest living baseball player. Astronaut Frank Borman made the announcement at a dinner honoring the players.

Neil Armstrong @CMDRApollo11
A mighty fine news update. But they neglected to inform us of the Dow Jones Industrial Index. Those of us on government salaries have to keep abreast of such things.

Bruce McCandless @BMCAPCOM
Some of our public affairs guys have shot off to get the goods on the stock market for the commander, or Czar, as the Russians are calling him.

Bruce McCandless @BMCAPCOM
We have looked into it for Neil. With respect to the Dow Jones Industrials, up to 1.05 p.m. Houston time there has been a net drop - minus 6 points on the industrial average.

Bruce McCandless @BMCAPCOM
Utilities have dropped 1.63 points and railroads dropped 1.58 points.

Neil Armstrong @CMDRApollo11
Not so good. Although Bruce tells us that we were responsible for the sharp rise in the overall Dow Jones

Index right after the stock market opened this morning.

Bruce McCandless @BMCAPCOM
Reading up the next midcourse correction coordinates to Apollo 11 now.

Bruce McCandless @BMCAPCOM
Also getting details back from Neil about the water in the suit issue they had earlier. We'll crank his information back into our engineering pipeline and see what we can come up with.

Bruce McCandless @BMCAPCOM
The biomed returns we're getting from Buzz continue to look kind of bad. When he moves around, they're cutting in and out. He needs to check the little electrical connector where it goes into the signal connector.

Buzz Aldrin @LMPApollo11
All the connections are about as tight as they can be. I'll take them off and put them on again and see if that makes any difference.

6 days 6 hours 56 minutes mission time

Bruce McCandless @BMCAPCOM
We're standing by for Columbia's mid-course correction burn. Everything's looking good from down here.

Buzz Aldrin @LMPApollo11
One minute 20 seconds to the burn.

Mike Collins @MCCMPPilot
4... 3... 2... 1... Burning.

Bruce McCandless @BMCAPCOM
Okay. Another successful burn completed. We're going to hand over the signal from Madrid station to Goldstone in 4 minutes. They may lose lock on the high-gain antenna at that time, but we have alternate pitch and yaw attitudes for them if they do.

Bruce McCandless @BMCAPCOM
We're still trying to work out the exact location of Apollo 11's landing site, Tranquility Base. We're thinking it is two-tenths of a kilometer west of West Crater, but we need to confirm that from actual observation.

Neil Armstrong @CMDRApollo11
I'm hoping that our 15mm film camera was working during the descent and we'll be able to confirm the touchdown point from the film.

Bruce McCandless @BMCAPCOM
Another thing we want to look into is what that laser light Buzz reported seeing during the ascent was, what color the beam was and where it emanated from.

Buzz Aldrin @LMPApollo11
The laser beam was mostly white with a tinge of yellow to it. It seemed to be coming from about a third of the way down to the Earth's shadow, on the light side of the Earth which was about two-thirds lit.

Neil Armstrong @CMDRApollo11
I saw the laser light too. It was a very bright spot of light and I confirm Buzz's observation of its position.

Neil Armstrong @CMDRApollo11
We're having an eating period now and my compliments to the chef. The food has been outstanding, and this cream of chicken soup is wonderful. I give it at least three 'spoons'.

Bruce McCandless @BMCAPCOM
Neil's culinary evaluations have been noted and they will be passed on for future reference - three spoons awarded for the cream of chicken soup.

Buzz Aldrin @LMPApollo11
Not all our food packets are liquid. We have a shrimp cocktail meal and this afternoon two of us enjoyed a very fine salmon salad.

Buzz Aldrin @LMPApollo11
Most of our food is prepared as bite-sized objects, designed to be able to go into the mouth all at once so as to avoid the problem of crumbs floating around the cabin.

Buzz Aldrin @LMPApollo11
On this flight, we've also carried along some pieces of bread and a ham spread. I'll try to show the folks back on Earth how easy it is to spread ham on bread while I'm in zero gravity.

Bruce McCandless @BMCAPCOM
We notice Apollo 11's roll rate increasing and have asked them to bring it down a little or we'll be losing contact through the high-gain antenna shortly.

Bruce McCandless @BMCAPCOM
We have lost contact with Apollo 11 and are now broadcasting in the blind. Asking them to contact us using the OMNI antenna.

Bruce McCandless @BMCAPCOM
Still broadcasting in the blind. No response from Apollo 11. Continuing to broadcast, waiting for an answer.

Michael Collins @CMPApollo11
We are calling using the high-gain antenna. No response so far.

Bruce McCandless @BMCAPCOM
We're back in contact with Apollo 11 now. That white-out lasted a full 30 minutes. Something we could well do without.

Bruce McCandless @BMCAPCOM
We have Mike coming through loud and clear on the high-gain antenna now. We were wondering what was up with those guys.

Michael Collins @CMPApollo11
It's all very quiet right now. We're just sitting here letting the thruster firing damp down. Nice to sit here and watch the Earth getting larger and larger and the Moon getting smaller and smaller.

Michael Collins @CMPApollo11
We have the Earth steady out of window 1, and the Moon steady out of window 3. The Sun is down below the lower equipment bay so it's not shining through the windows and heating the place up.

Michael Collins @CMPApollo11
As long as the thermal people in Houston are happy, we're happy.

Bruce McCandless @BMCAPCOM
We are about ready to start establishing the passive thermal control, but need to send up some high-gain antenna angles, so we need to know if Mike will be spinning Columbia in a positive or negative direction.

Michael Collins @CMPApollo11
I could spin either way. I had planned spinning in the positive direction.

Bruce McCandless @BMCAPCOM
For spinning the spacecraft positive, the high-gain antenna setting should be pitch plus 30, yaw 270.

6 days 9 hours 45 minutes mission time

Bruce McCandless @BMCAPCOM
Passive thermal control has now been established. The Green Team is now signing off and the friendly White Team commentator is taking over.

Charlie Duke @CDCAPCOM
White Team is now on and standing by for an exciting evening of TV and a pre-sleep report.

Neil Armstrong @CMDRApollo11
We're sending down TV of the receding Moon and the Earth as we draw closer. Unfortunately, Houston is reporting that the pictures are not good.

Neil Armstrong @CMDRApollo11
We know there are a lot of scientists from a lot of countries standing by to examine our lunar samples, so we thought we'd send down some TV of how they are stored onboard.

Neil Armstrong @CMDRApollo11
I'm trying to show the Moon rock samples which are in vacuum-packed containers that were closed in a vacuum on the lunar surface, sealed and then brought inside the lunar module.

Neil Armstrong @CMDRApollo11
The samples were then put inside fiber glass bags, zippered, re-sealed and placed into special containers on the side of the command module. Hope the pictures are a little better now.

Buzz Aldrin @LMPApollo11
It's worth noting that the fears of many soil scientists and geologists that the lunar rock and soil samples would burst into flames when exposed to the air inside Eagle proved unfounded... fortunately for us.

Charlie Duke @CDCAPCOM
We've got a pretty dark picture on all our screens down here. Neil needs to check his f-stop and see if he can open it up a little bit.

Buzz Aldrin @LMPApollo11
Our little monitor in the cabin is showing a very bright picture.

Neil Armstrong @CMDRApollo11
We're down around f-4, which we thought would be plenty light. Well, we'll open it up a little more.

Charlie Duke @CDCAPCOM
A much better picture is coming down from inside the spacecraft now. In fact, it's excellent.

Michael Collins @CMPApollo11
I've just performed a series of simple experiments to demonstrate to the kids on Earth how stuff behaves in zero gravity. Particularly how water behaves.

Michael Collins @CMPApollo11
Next, I'll demonstrate the water gun. People can see how we are able to drink water without any gas in it—filtered water. We just put the nozzle in our mouth and pull the trigger to get it started. Simple.

Charlie Duke @CDCAPCOM
Mike just asked me if I can see the picture of Earth he's sending down. This time, I refused to bite having misidentified the Earth for the Moon a while back.

Neil Armstrong @CMDRApollo11
If the image they're seeing at Mission Control is getting larger, that means it is the place we are coming home to. No matter where you travel, it's always nice to get home.

Charlie Duke @CDCAPCOM
That was a good show and excellent demonstrations for the kids. We thank the crew of Apollo 11 very much.

Michael Collins @CMPApollo11
We've had the morning news today, but I've asked Houston if they could also prepare a brief summary of the evening news for us. I'd hate to miss anything that might be going on down there.

Charlie Duke @CDCAPCOM
We have a flurry of activity right now over in the
public affairs pit with people scrambling to get
together an evening news update for Mike and the
Apollo 11 crew. Who knew the crew were still so tuned
in to earthly affairs?

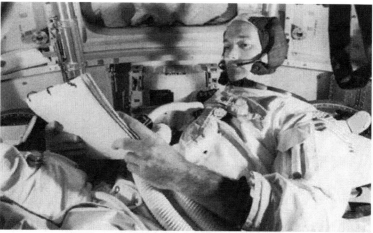

Mike Collins inside Columbia

Buzz Aldrin @LMPApollo11
We just had a bit of an anecdotal local weather report
from Charlie Duke. Seems they've been having a good
bit of rain in Houston today. Looking out of the
window here, I can see it's pretty overcast down over
the Antarctic ice cap too.

Michael Collins @CMPApollo11
Love Buzz's last comment to Charlie about the
weather on Earth. How about that for one-upmanship?

Charlie Duke @CDCAPCOM
The weather in the recovery area in the Pacific looks
pretty good as far as we can tell. There are a few
clouds on the weather map I'm looking at here, but

nothing of any great significance. Looks like it's going to be real nice for recovery.

Buzz Aldrin @LMPApollo11
Looks like the navy called in good weather and calm seas for our re-entry. We'll get a good look at actual conditions when we splash down tomorrow. We'll be giving it a pretty close eye.

Charlie Duke @CDCAPCOM
We're looking at Buzz's biomed readouts and we're still not getting anything. We want him to temporarily disconnect all 3 sensors and connectors from his body and re-attach them in a different configuration. Looks like there's a broken lead somewhere.

Buzz Aldrin @LMPApollo11
I've been fiddling with the biomed connectors, trying to re-connect them. Meanwhile, I believe I can simply show the Houston medics through the TV link that my heart is in fact still working.

Buzz Aldrin @LMPApollo11
I think the problem was that the center lead dried out. I've put on the new one and we'll see how that works. It felt real good to have these annoying medical sensors off my body even if only temporarily.

Charlie Duke @CDCAPCOM
All the biomed sensors are sending down good data now. The medics have sent a big thank you up to the crew of Apollo 11.

Charlie Duke @CDCAPCOM
Based on our sighting since the midcourse correction burn, we now have preliminary tracking with more coming in. We think we can tweak it so Apollo 11

comes in right in the center of the corridor for re-entry.

Charlie Duke @CDCAPCOM
President Nixon, as he prepares to fly out to greet the astronauts, has predicted that within 31 years, man will have visited at least one other planet bearing some form of life.

Charlie Duke @CDCAPCOM
The president made that prediction before a group of foreign exchange students visiting the White House - interplanetary missions by the year 2000. Great!

Neil Armstrong @CMDRApollo11
All three of us up here fervently hope that the president's prediction of interplanetary missions by the year 2000 comes to pass.

Charlie Duke @CDCAPCOM
The president also conferred today with Chairman Eric Wheeler of the Joint Chiefs of Staff on his return from Vietnam.

Charlie Duke @CDCAPCOM
The Flight Surgeon is right up out of his chair. The monitor is showing Buzz's hearbeat to be way, way up!

Charlie Duke @CDCAPCOM
Turns out there's a good reason... Buzz is exercising.

Michael Collins @CMPApollo11
Good that Buzz gave White Team something to get excited about.

Michael Collins @CMPApollo11
There's not a lot going on right now, and I can just visualize them all sitting around in Mission Control with their feet on the consoles relaxing and drinking coffee.

Charlie Duke @CDCAPCOM
Mike must have X-ray, telescopic eyes. He sure can see a long way.

Michael Collins @CMPApollo11
My X-ray, telescopic eyes are showing me just two people in the viewing room at Mission Control, and that is more than in the trench.

Charlie Duke @CDCAPCOM
Mike's not far off. There are only eight people in the viewing room and just six in the trench right now. However, it is two in the morning and there's not a lot happening.

Charlie Duke @CDCAPCOM
The highlight of the shift has been Buzz startling the flight surgeon out of his chair with his unannounced exercise routine.

Charlie Duke @CDCAPCOM
While we're in a quiet period, I've asked Neil to give us his onboard readouts of batteries and the reaction control system.

Charlie Duke @CDCAPCOM
Batteries seem to be in good shape. We're about to read up some detailed re-entry coordinates, procedures and star settings for re-entry. No point in noting all of them here, except that the procedures assume no mid-course correction 6.

Charlie Duke @CDCAPCOM
Set stars for re-entry preparations will be the stars Daneb and Vega. We're in the process of handing over the signal to Honeysuckle Station. Handover will be 2 minutes from now.

Buzz Aldrin @LMPApollo11
Just said goodnight to Charlie and his sleepy White Team who are going off-shift now. We're sleepy too, but not as sleepy as last night after yesterday's action-packed events.

NO CONTACT FOR 10 HOURS 34 MINUTES

7 days 2 hours 59 minutes mission time

Owen Garriott @OGCAPCOM
The crew of Apollo 11 seems to have had a real good night's sleep - up to 10 hours with no exchanges and none needed. We just wished them a good morning and noted that voice comms is cutting out intermittingly.

Buzz Aldrin @LMPApollo11
Houston has just confirmed that mid-course correction burn number 6 has been cancelled. We need to charge Battery B and do a wastewater dump a little differently this time - on their marks from the ground.

Owen Garriott @OGCAPCOM
We want the wastewater dump to be at a time which will enable the ship to hold its proper configuration - in about 15 or 20 minutes. On our mark, we'd like a wastewater dump down to 40%.

Buzz Aldrin @LMPApollo11
Owen and his team must have stayed up all night figuring this one out. I'm handing the display and keyboard back over to Houston now.

Owen Garriott @OGCAPCOM
We've changed the wastewater dump to 45% remaining. That should let Apollo 11 arrive at Earth interface with just about a full load of waste water.

Michael Collins @CMPApollo11
We have now dumped wastewater to 45% and Houston concurs.

Owen Garriott @OGCAPCOM
The weather forecast in the recovery area shows acceptable conditions. Two thousand foot high scattered clouds, wind 13 knots, visibility 10 miles.

Owen Garriott @OGCAPCOM
Recovery area is now expected to be just a little ways north of the intertropical convergence zone, which the crew can probably see right now if they look out of their windows.

7 days 5 hours 35 minutes mission time

Neil Armstrong @CMDRApollo11
We've had no contact with Houston for a couple of hours now. No need. So they've interrupted our repose and alerted us that they now have the most recent news update prepared and available for our listening pleasure.

Owen Garriott @OGCAPCOM
Here is the news for the Apollo 11 crew: Prince Juan Carlos was formally designated today to become General Franco's successor and eventual king of Spain.

Owen Garriott @OGCAPCOM
South Korea's first super highway, linking the capital Seoul with the port of Incheon has been named 'the Apollo Highway' in honor of the Apollo 11 mission.

Owen Garriott @OGCAPCOM
President Nixon has started on his round the world trip. Today, he is in San Francisco on his first stop which will take him onto the USS Hornet from where he will watch the return to Earth of Apollo 11 and greet the crew.

Owen Garriott @OGCAPCOM
The president plans to visit seven nations during his trip. Like the crew of Apollo 11, he had to miss the All Star baseball game which was rained out. It will be played later today.

Owen Garriott @OGCAPCOM
The residents of all major West Coast cities plan to turn on all their lights between 9 p.m. and midnight tonight to make them visible to the Apollo 11 crew.

Owen Garriott @OGCAPCOM
The crew should be able to see porch lights, store lights, Christmas lights and whatever other lights may be turned on.

Owen Garriott @OGCAPCOM
A couple in Tennessee have named their newborn baby daughter 'Module'. The mother said she had

balked at her husband's suggestion of 'Lunar Module' since it didn't sound so good. So they compromised and named the baby girl Module.

Michael Collins @CMPApollo11
Good luck to the young lady with that name. The latest update from the crew here is that we have just finished breakfast. I had sliced peaches, sausage patties, two cups of coffee, and I forget what else.

Owen Garriott @OGCAPCOM
Mike's breakfast sounded pretty good. As a matter of fact, I'm way overdue for a meal here. I could use some of that space food myself.

Michael Collins @CMPApollo11
We've been doing a little culinary flight planning for the next mission, Apollo 12. We're trying to calculate the maximum amount of spaghetti and meatballs we could get on board for lunar module pilot Al Bean.

Owen Garriott @OGCAPCOM
I'm not sure any of our current spacecraft could accommodate the volume and weight of consumables Mike may be considering for Apollo 12. However, we will have EECOM look into it as well.

Owen Garriott @OGCAPCOM
The medics at the console next to me have informed me that the shrew is an animal that can eat six times its own body weight every 24 hours. This may be a satisfactory baseline for Mike and EECOM's calculations regarding Al Bean's consumables for the Apollo 12 mission.

Michael Collins @CMPApollo11
Talking about EECOM, it was quite a bit colder in here last night than on any previous night. We're wondering if EECOM noticed any change in the data or explanation for that.

Owen Garriott @OGCAPCOM
Temperatures are looking good from down here. Lowest temperature recorded was 40 degrees.

Owen Garriott @OGCAPCOM
Further checks indicate that cabin temperatures may have cooled down perhaps 2 or 3 degrees in the past 24 hours.

Owen Garriott @OGCAPCOM
I'm turning things over to Bruce McCandless, the Green Team CAPCOM, at this time. I will see the Apollo 11 crew on the ground tomorrow. That will be quite a day! Quite a celebration!

Michael Collins @CMPApollo11
I thanked Owen and the Purple/Maroon Team for the great job they have done in assisting Apollo 11. And Buzz has chipped in to say their efforts have been greatly appreciated up here.

Bruce McCandless @BMCAPCOM
I'm back in the CAPCOM chair now. With reference to Mike's subjective observation about the cooler temperature, we can report that we did see a drop of about 3 degrees.

Bruce McCandless @BMCAPCOM
It appears Apollo 10 reported the same subjective observations during the translunar and transearth phases.

Bruce McCandless @BMCAPCOM
I'm about to go over the re-entry procedures and parameters checklist with the Apollo 11 crew now. This will take quite a while – it's very detailed.

Bruce McCandless @BMCAPCOM
Meanwhile, I've informed the crew of Apollo 11 that the All Star game has just ended with the National League winning 9 to 3 over American.

NO CONTACT FOR 1 HOUR 7 MINUTES

Neil Armstrong @CMDRApollo11
We have gone through, completed and read back a whole slew of re-entry settings page by detailed page. Houston now tells us we are now just 95,970 miles out from Earth - practically back in our own back yard.

Bruce McCandless @BMCAPCOM
Current velocity of Apollo 11 is 5,991 feet per second. Neil, Buzz and Mike are about to send down some historic TV and commentary for public viewing worldwide – and it really is worldwide.

Neil Armstrong @CMDRApollo11
A hundred years ago, Jules Verne wrote a book about a voyage to the Moon. His spaceship, Columbia, took off from Florida and landed back in the Pacific Ocean after the mission.

Neil Armstrong @CMDRApollo11
It seems appropriate to us to share today some of the reflections of the crew as the modern day Columbia completes its rendezvous with the planet Earth tomorrow.

Bruce McCandless @BMCAPCOM
Damn! We have loss of signal here. Working to get it back.

Bruce McCandless @BMCAPCOM
Okay. We have the TV signal back. The crew can continue with their transmission.

Michael Collins @CMPApollo11
This trip of ours to the Moon may have looked simple or easy. I can assure everyone that has not been the case.

Michael Collins @CMPApollo11
The Saturn V rocket which put us into orbit is an incredibly complicated piece of machinery. Fortunately, every piece of the machine worked flawlessly.

Michael Collins @CMPApollo11
The computer up above my head has a 38,000 word vocabulary, each word of which has been carefully chosen to be of the utmost value to us. For every piece of equipment to perform flawlessly, a massive quality control effort was undertaken.

Michael Collins @CMPApollo11
Had the engines on the lunar module failed to perform, Neil and Buzz would have been stuck on the lunar surface with no hope of rescue.

Michael Collins @CMPApollo11
Our large rocket engine on the aft end of our service module had to perform flawlessly, or we would have been stuck in lunar orbit.

Michael Collins @CMPApollo11
Tomorrow, the heat shield on the re-entry vehicle must hold to protect us from the searing heat of re-entry and the parachutes above my head must work perfectly or we will plunge into the ocean at a fatal velocity.

Michael Collins @CMPApollo11
We have always had confidence that this equipment will work, and work properly. We continue to have confidence that it will do so for the remainder of the flight.

Michael Collins @CMPApollo11
All this is possible only through the blood, sweat and tears of thousands. First, the American workmen who put these pieces of machinery together in the factory.

Michael Collins @CMPApollo11
Second, the painstaking work done by the various test teams during assembly and retest after assembly.

Michael Collins @CMPApollo11
Finally, the people at the Manned Spacecraft Center: management, mission planning, flight control and crew training. We thank them all.

Michael Collins @CMPApollo11
This operation is somewhat like the periscope of a submarine. All you see is the three of us. But beneath the surface, there are thousands and thousands of others, and to all of those I would like to say, "Thank you very much."

7 days 9 hours 38 minutes mission time

Bruce McCandless @BMCAPCOM
We're getting a good picture of Buzz now, but no voice modulation. We're working on that. Also, Neil needs to open up the f-stop on the TV camera. Maybe to f-22.

Bruce McCandless @BMCAPCOM
Okay. We're finally getting good sound. Buzz can go ahead now.

Buzz Aldrin @LMPApollo11
We feel that this mission stands as a symbol of the insatiable curiosity of all mankind to explore the unknown. Neil's statement upon setting foot on the surface of the Moon for the first time sums up our feelings quite nicely.

Buzz Aldrin @LMPApollo11
Neil said, "This is a small step for (a) man, but a giant leap for mankind." We accepted the challenge of going to the Moon because the acceptance of this challenge was inevitable in mankind's forward movement.

Buzz Aldrin @LMPApollo11
We've been particularly pleased with the call signs that we laboriously chose for our spacecrafts, Columbia and Eagle; and with the emblem of the flight - the U.S. eagle bringing the symbol of peace (the olive branch) from the Earth to the Moon.

The Apollo 11 emblem: eagle with olive branch

Buzz Aldrin @LMPApollo11
It was our unanimous choice to deposit and leave the olive branch symbol on the Moon to reflect the fact that 'we came in peace for all mankind.' Personally, in reflecting on the mission, a verse from Psalms comes to my mind.

Buzz Aldrin @LMPApollo11
"When I consider the heavens, the work of Thy fingers, the Moon and the stars which Thou has ordained, what is man that Thou art mindful of him?"

Neil Armstrong @CMDRApollo11
The responsibility for the success so far of this flight lies first with history and the giants of science who preceded this effort; next with the American people, who have through their will, indicated their desire for such an effort.

Neil Armstrong @CMDRApollo11
Next, to four U.S. administrations and their Congresses for implementing the collective will of the

people. We would like to give a special thanks to all those Americans who designed, constructed and tested the technology needed for such an endeavor.

Neil Armstrong @CMDRApollo11
Those engineers, technicians and administrators put all of their heart and abilities into this effort. To those people tonight, we give a special thank you.

Bruce McCandless @BMCAPCOM
I have a flight plan update and some re-entry photography information ready to send up to Apollo 11.

Bruce McCandless @BMCAPCOM
If they are going to use a fresh magazine of color interior film to capture the fireball surrounding the capsule as it plunges through the atmosphere, we recommend f-11 at 1/250, 1/60 of a second at 6 frames per second.

Bruce McCandless @BMCAPCOM
They should focus on 50 feet as the parachutes open. However, if they are going to use a film magazine that has already been partly used for interior shots, the settings will need to be different.

Neil Armstrong @CMDRApollo11
I have the camera settings noted down. We are going to use a fresh magazine for our fiery re-entry, and it will be color interior film.

Neil Armstrong @CMDRApollo11
We're thinking that we might want to run some of that at 12 frames per second, which would give us 7.8 minutes. Maybe then just an occasional burst at 12 frames per second and the rest at 6.

Bruce McCandless @BMCAPCOM
Neil's plan looks fine to us down here. We just now
need to go through some stowage procedures prior to
re-entry.

Bruce McCandless @BMCAPCOM
Neil has noted down all the stowage procedures, so
it's time for the friendly Green Team to go off for the
night, and off for the last time.

Bruce McCandless @BMCAPCOM
We wish Apollo 11 and its crew a good night and
Godspeed for a successful re-entry.

Neil Armstrong @CMDRApollo11
We appreciate all the fine work done by the Green
Team and we'll be sure to thank them in person when
we get back.

Michael Collins @CMPApollo11
Buzz and I would like to add how much we too have
really enjoyed working with all those Greenies.

Bruce McCandless @BMCAPCOM
They're all smiles down here in Mission Control,
Houston, maybe also a little teary-eyed, even those
dour numbers guys in the trench.

Bruce McCandless @BMCAPCOM
Meanwhile, I'm still on and Mike's biomed sensors are
still showing erratic traces – connected...
disconnected... connected. Looks like he's sending us a
coded message of some sort.

Michael Collins @CMPApollo11
I've promised Bruce I will be sure to let him know if I stop breathing.

Bruce McCandless @BMCAPCOM
The trace on Mikes respiration rate is still flat. Before he turns in this evening, he might try putting some fresh paste on the biomed sensors that go on the side of his lower rib cage.

Bruce McCandless @BMCAPCOM
However, if that doesn't work, the medics have agreed to forget about it.

Bruce McCandless @BMCAPCOM
In the flight plan, we have the crew commencing a sleep period at 182 hours. Neil has confirmed that they will be sticking to the flight plan pretty much.

Bruce McCandless @BMCAPCOM
We'll have a landing area weather update ready for them shortly.

Neil Armstrong @CMDRApollo11
We plan to be looking out the windows and watching the lights folks in the northwest corner of the U.S. will be turning on for our enjoyment. Other than that, we'll be on the flight plan.

Bruce McCandless @BMCAPCOM
At about 180 hours 45 minutes, well be handing over from Goldstone to Honeysuckle so there may be temporary loss of signal. I'm about to hand over my CAPCOM chair and will see the crew when they get back.

Bruce McCandless @BMCAPCOM
Charlie Duke is up next in the CAPCOM chair.

7 days 13 hours 43 minutes mission time

Charlie Duke @CDCAPCOM
We need to terminate battery B charge at this time. Also, we see the weather is clobbering our targeted landing point with scattered thunderstorms. We don't want to tangle with one of those.

Charlie Duke @CDCAPCOM
After much discussion, we have decided to move Apollo 11's aim point substantially downrange. I've sent the new coordinates up to Neil. The weather in the new area is super with 10 mile visibility and 6 foot waves. USS Hornet is sitting in great position to get to the new area.

Michael Collins @CMPApollo11
Seems we'll now be landing quite a bit closer to Hawaii. That has to be good news. I like it.

Charlie Duke @CDCAPCOM
We had earlier told the crew that during re-entry they should set the camera at 50 feet. It turns out that the biggest number on the camera dial is 25 feet. So they should just set it to infinity and leave it there.

Charlie Duke @CDCAPCOM
If the crew can now verify that they have changed the CO_2 canister, then read us the battery and PYRO levels, we will be ready to send them to bed.

Charlie Duke @CDCAPCOM
We just got word a moment ago that McDonald Observatory has been able to pick up the spacecraft

on their telescope. Neil said he had been looking out for their laser. I'm thinking that was a joke, right?

Neil Armstrong @CMDRApollo11
All stowage done. CO_2 canister changed. PYRO and battery levels read down to Houston. Ready now to bed down for the night.

Charlie Duke @CDCAPCOM
Just said goodnight to the crew from the White Team for the last time. It's been a beautiful show from all three of those guys. We'll see them after they get out of their quarantine on USS Hornet.

NO CONTACT FOR 7 HOURS 20 MINUTES 19 SECONDS

7 days 21 hours 41 minutes mission time

Ronald Evans @RECAPCOM
Just settled into my CAPCOM chair with the rest of the Maroon Team taking up their positions and checking the current status of Apollo 11 systems and the crew.

Ronald Evans @RECAPCOM
The crew of Apollo 11 are up and about, probably eating breakfast, even though we had intended to let them sleep until 190 hours. We are able to inform them that midcourse correction burn 7 is no longer required.

Neil Armstrong @CMDRApollo11
Ron says he has the 'Maroon Bugle' ready to read up to us. We are all ears.

Ronald Evans @RECAPCOM
Apollo 11 remains the prime story today with the world awaiting the landing today at about 11.49 a.m. Houston Time. President Nixon surprised the astronauts' wives with a phone call from San Francisco just before he boarded a plane to fly out to meet the crew.

Ronald Evans @RECAPCOM
In Washington, House tax reformers have fashioned a provision that would make it impossible for wealthy individuals to avoid tax entirely through tax-free investments of special allowances. Everyone would pay taxes on at least half their income.

Neil Armstrong @CMDRApollo11
I need Ron to hold on a minute. Got to fix something floating around the cabin. Okay, caught it and stowed it away. Ready to listen to the rest of the 'Maroon Team Bugle' now.

Ronald Evans @RECAPCOM
The research submarine Ben Franklin, which is studying the Gulf Stream, set a record by descending to just 10 feet above the ocean floor off the Georgia coast. The mission is led by Jacques Picard.

Ronald Evans @RECAPCOM
Air Canada says it has accepted 2,300 new reservations for flights to the Moon in the past 5 days. It might be noted that over 100 of the reservations have been made by men for their mothers-in-law.

Ronald Evans @RECAPCOM
It appears the Moon mission has inspired hundreds of songwriters, and Nashville reports it is being flooded

with Moon songs. The song at the top of the best sellers list this week is, "In the Year 2525".

Neil Armstrong @CMDRApollo11
Very interesting news update from the Maroon Team. We thank them for that. Looking at upcoming procedures here, it looks like we're not going to be able to get quite back on the flight plan. Not quite, just about though.

Ronald Evans @RECAPCOM
The weather forecast in the landing area right now is for wind at 18 knots, visibility 10 miles, 3 to 6-foot waves. It looks like Apollo 11 will be landing about 10 minutes before sunrise.

Ronald Evans @RECAPCOM
Sending up a great deal of re-entry settings and procedures to Apollo 11 now. Too much, too technical and too detailed to be useful to note down here. Nothing of general interest, but of crucial interest to the crew.

Jim Lovell @JLCMDApollo11Backup
As commander of the backup crew, I've sent Neil a message reminding him that the most difficult part of the mission is going to be after recovery.

Michael Collins @CMPApollo11
The Earth is really large in our windows now and, of course, we see a crescent. We've been taking pictures and we have just four exposures to go on this camera. We'll take those and then pack that camera.

Ronald Evans @RECAPCOM
A little recovery force information: The USS Hornet is now on station, just far enough off the target point to keep from getting hit. The chopper Recovery 1 is on station there.

Ronald Evans @RECAPCOM
Hawaii Rescue 1 and 2, and the C-130, are within 40 minutes of the target point.

Ronald Evans @RECAPCOM
We are now showing about 1 hour and 37 minutes from re-entry interface.

Ronald Evans @RECAPCOM
We are recommending the left VHF antenna from now on. And as Apollo 11's backup command module pilot,

I am reminding Mike Collins to re-enter the Earth's atmosphere BEF (blunt end forward).

Neil Armstrong @CMDRApollo11
We have completed the guidance platform realignment and passed our sextant star check at entry attitude. Right now, we're maneuvering to our horizon pitch attitude.

Ronald Evans @RECAPCOM
Uh, oh! We have lost data from Apollo 11 – the last thing we need at this stage of the mission!

Ronald Evans @RECAPCOM
A lot of tense red faces here at Mission Control. We lost data with Apollo 11 for quite a while there during this critical final phase. Thank goodness it's back now.

8 days 1 hour 58 minutes mission time (1 hour and 34 minutes from re-entry)

Michael Collins @CMPApollo11
We can see the Earth passing by the window. It looks like what I consider to be the correct size and shape. Doesn't seem to have changed too much since we left.

Buzz Aldrin @LMPApollo11
I'm seeing a loss of signal strength on the OMNI C antenna.

Ronald Evans @RECAPCOM
We recommend switching to OMNI B antenna... or at least a better one than C. We lost all data from Apollo 11 a while back, causing a lot of anxious red faces here.

Neil Armstrong @CMDRApollo11
We have completed the P52 (guidance platform realignment) and passed our sextant star check at re-entry attitude. Right now, we're maneuvering to our first horizon check, pitch attitude of 298 degrees.

Ronald Evans @RECAPCOM
The crew have indicated that a command module pre-heat prior to re-entry will not be necessary. We don't want them to jettison the hydrogen tank that stratified. They should just stir up the tank – hydrogen tank 2.

Michael Collins @CMPApollo11
Giving the tanks the occasional stir is no problem. Command module Columbia has taken real good care of us, and we're doing everything we can to take good care of her in return. The old lady has been a champ!

Ronald Evans @RECAPCOM
Handing back the computer to Apollo 11. It looks like they're coming into VHF range so we are trying a VHF check. Sending the VHF signal up to them now.

Buzz Aldrin @LMPApollo11
The VHF signal is coming through loud and clear and Houston report they are hearing us fine too. So, hopefully no more comms problems from now on in.

Ronald Evans @RECAPCOM
Apollo 11 is now GO for PYRO ARM, and command module pressurization looks mighty fine to us. Command module RCS (reaction control system) also looks good.

Ronald Evans @RECAPCOM
Weather is still holding real fine in the landing area. High, scattered clouds, and still 3 to 6 foot waves. Thirty-three minutes to re-entry interface.

Michael Collins @CMPApollo11
The Sun seems to be going down on schedule. It's getting real dark in here.

Ronald Evans @RECAPCOM
We see the crew getting ready for separation from the service module. Everything looks mighty fine down here.

Jules Bergman @JBNBCNews
Just a few minutes from now, the spacecraft will soar in over the southern hemisphere. It will pass over Australia, hit the splashdown area and hopefully come in for a good landing 950 miles southwest of Hawaii.
Jules Bergman @JBNBCNews
When the spacecraft hits the Earth's atmosphere, it has to fly in heatshield first at precisely a 6.5 degree flight path angle.

Jules Bergman @JBNBCNews
The danger here is that if the spaceship enters too steeply, it will burn up in the atmosphere and the crew will be lost.

Jules Bergman @JBNBCNews
On the other hand, if the spaceship flies in too shallow, it will skip off the atmosphere, go back into space and no recovery will be possible.

Neil Armstrong @CMDRApollo11
Mike is on the controls about to initiate separation, after which we will have the re-entry vehicle aligned and ready to re-enter the Earth's atmosphere.

Michael Collins @CMPApollo11
Arming for separation in 4... 3... 2... 1...

Neil Armstrong @CMDRApollo11
We have service module separation.

Ronald Evans @RECAPCOM
We confirm service module separation. Apollo 11 is now cleared for landing.

Michael Collins @CMPApollo11
We appreciate Houston's clearance for landing. Landing gear down and locked.

Michael Collins @CMPApollo11
That's a joke guys!

Neil Armstrong @CMDRApollo11
We have the service module going by. A little high and a little bit to the right. It's rotating just like it should be and thrusters are firing.

RE-ENTRY

8 days 3 hours 3 minutes mission time

Ronald Evans @RECAPCOM
Apollo 11 will be hitting re-entry interface just about...just about... NOW!

Neil Armstrong @CMDRApollo11
Okay here we go! Mike has it. We are hitting re-entry interface and cutting a path through Earth's atmosphere to the landing area.

Walter Cronkite @WCCBSNews
This is the most tense time — waiting to hear if the astronauts have made it through the fiery re-entry safely.

Wally Schirra @WSNASA
As the capsule plunges through the atmosphere surrounded by luminous plasma, radio communication is no longer possible.

Walter Cronkite @WCCBSNews
If all has gone well, Apollo 11 should be coming out of radio blackout just about now.

Ronald Evans @RECAPCOM
Standing by for a DSKY (display and keyboard) reading from Apollo 11 as it continues its descent through the atmosphere.

Ronald Evans @RECAPCOM
Continuing to stand by to hear from Apollo 11.

Ronald Evans @RECAPCOM
Standing by.

USS Hornet @USSHornet
Trying to contact Apollo 11. No response so far.

USS Hornet @USSHornet
Still no response.

Ronald Evans @RECAPCOM
Oh, boy! We are receiving a confirmation of visual sighting of Apollo 11. Drogue parachutes have been deployed. Standing by.

USS Hornet @USSHornet
Trying to contact Apollo 11. No response so far.

USS Hornet @USSHornet
Still trying.

Neil Armstrong @CMDRApollo11
We are reading USS Hornet loud and clear! Our position is 1330, 16915.

Neil Armstrong @CMDRApollo11
We are at 4,000... now 3,500 feet. Parachutes deployed... descending slowly.

USS Hornet @USSHornet
We copy Apollo 11 on voice, descending on chutes at 2,500 feet... now 1,500 feet.

Swim Team 1 @ST1USSHornet
I have a visual on Apollo 11. About one mile dead ahead.

Neil Armstrong @CMDRApollo11
300 feet.

Swim Team 1 @ST1USSHornet
The spacecraft and its chutes are looking real good.

RECOVERY

8 days 3 hours 18 minutes mission time

Swim Team 1 @ST1USSHornet
Splashdown! We observe splashdown of Apollo 11 at
this time!

Mission controllers upon receiving news of the successful splashdown

Jules Bergman @JBNBCNews
The flight of Apollo 11 is over. The men are on the ocean. There has been word from Mike Collins inside the capsule. He says, "The crew is in excellent shape." The recovery helicopters are moving in now.

David Brinkley @DBABCNews
Mission controllers in Houston are standing and cheering wildly at the sight of Apollo 11 splashing down on time and on target in the Pacific ocean.

Walter Cronkite @WCCBSNews
They've made it! The crew of Apollo 11 are back on Earth—at least the watery part of it.

Jules Bergman @JBNBCNews
The helicopter crew tasked with recovering the astronauts are carrying sets of biological isolation garments. The swimmers will open the capsule hatch and throw in the special garments for the astronauts to put on.

Jules Bergman @JBNBCNews
The astronauts will be assisted into two 7-man life rafts where they will wait to be hoisted into the main recovery helicopter.

Wally Schirra @WSCBSNews
The re-entry vehicle is reported to be 'Stable 2'. That means upside down but not sinking. The three inflatable bags will bring it upright. The floatation collar will rule out any chance of it sinking.

Jules Bergman @JBNBCNews
Recovery helicopter Navy 66 is above the capsule now, and we see one of the swimmers jumping from the helicopter now. Also decontamination dispensers and extra scuba tanks being dropped.

Wally Schirra @WSCBSNews
One swimmer is already in the life raft and we can see Navy UDT swimmer Lieutenant Clancy Hatleberg standing in the chopper's hatch ready to jump.

Wally Schirra @WSCBSNews
In the early days of the Mercury program, splashdown distances were so far apart from where the recovery vehicles were.

Wally Schirra @WSCBSNews
Now we have spaceships travelling half a million miles through space and splashing down within 15 miles of the recovery ship. Incredible!

Wally Schirra @WSCBSNews
The helicopters were there immediately. They were never out of sight of the spacecraft even as it descended. The swimmers were in the water immediately, getting the floatation collar around the capsule.

Ronald Evans @RECAPCOM
We will continue to monitor for any conversation between the spacecraft and recovery forces, but we will not initiate a call from now on to the spacecraft from here at Mission Control.

Ronald Evans @RECAPCOM
It's down to the USS Hornet now.

Jules Bergman @JBNBCNews
Just one step remaining in the mission now. That is to get the astronauts safely aboard the USS Hornet. Once there, they will enter the portable quarantine facility, be checked out by the NASA doctor and have a brief conversation with the president.

Jules Bergman @JBNBCNews
The president will remain outside the onboard quarantine facility of course. He will only see the astronauts through a small viewing panel and communicate with them through a microphone and speakers set up.

Jules Bergman @JBNBCNews
Lieutenant Clancy Hatleberg is now opening the hatch of the re-entry vehicle. We can see him throwing the three isolation garments into the spacecraft and closing the hatch once more.

Wally Schirra @WSCBSNews
Two of the astronauts are coming now out of the capsule and into the life raft.

Wally Schirra @WSCBSNews
The sea is a little rough here - three to six foot waves, winds about 18 knots and there's a good deal of

bobbing up and down both of the spacecraft and the life rafts.

Jules Bergman @JBNBCNews
After some difficulty and some help from one of the astronauts in closing the capsule hatch, Lieutenant Hatleberg is now spraying the hatchway on the spacecraft. This is all part of the detailed decontamination procedures for this mission.

Jules Bergman @JBNBCNews
All three astronauts are now in the raft right alongside the space capsule. 100 feet away at the end of a tether, and with an anchor to stabilize it, is another raft with the frogmen who had installed the floatation collar around the capsule.

Jules Bergman @JBNBCNews
The three astronauts and Lieutenant Hatleberg are decontaminating each other with special disinfectant.

They need to be very careful while moving around and doing that that they don't flip that raft over.

Wally Schirra @WSCBSNews
We had a raft flip over on Apollo 9. That was quite a scary moment. The Apollo 11 crew have to be quite agile there in that raft getting themselves scrubbed down while maintaining their balance and the stability of the life raft.

Jules Bergman @JBNBCNews
The first astronaut is climbing into the cage now, about to be hoisted up into the helicopter.

Jules Bergman @JBNBCNews
After all three astronauts are off the life raft, Lieutenant Hatleberg will conclude the decontamination and safety procedures involved in this stage of the recovery.

Wally Schirra @WSCBSNews
Once the astronauts are inside the helicopter and Hatleberg has completed his decontamination procedures, he will remove his garment – the one designed to keep bugs from getting in.

Wally Schirra @WSCBSNews
Hatleberg will leave his garment on the raft along with all the chemical materials, and then sink the raft to the bottom of the ocean.

Wally Schirra @WSCBSNews
Lieutenant Hatleberg will then swim to the second raft at the end of the 100-foot tether. The first astronaut is now being winched up into recovery helicopter No. 66.

Wally Schirra @WSCBSNews
The second astronaut is now going up. We don't know yet which of the crew have been the first ones into the helicopter.

Wally Schirra @WSCBSNews
There goes the third astronaut.

Wally Schirra @WSCBSNews
There seems to be a problem. The basket containing the third astronaut appears to have frozen, no longer moving up. It is just suspended below the helicopter being buffeted around by these fairly strong winds.

Wally Schirra @WSCBSNews
Okay. They have the winch working once more. The third astronaut, who we believe to be Neil Armstrong is about to climb out of the cage and into the helicopter.

Wally Schirra @WSCBSNews
Now all three Apollo 11 astronauts are aboard recovery helicopter 66, the door is closed and they are heading back to the Hornet.

Jules Bergman @JBABCNews
We can see the president and his secret service detail on the admiral's bridge of the Hornet intently following the recovery. It's starting to rain now, but there is an overhang above the president so he's not getting wet.

Jules Bergman @JBABCNews
The president is now about to move off the bridge, possibly down to the hanger deck where he will greet the returning crew of Apollo 11.

Walter Cronkite @WCCBSNews
Here comes recovery helicopter 66 landing on the deck of the USS Hornet bringing with them a most, most valuable cargo – the three astronauts of the successful Apollo 11 mission. What a moment!

David Brinkley @BNBCNews
This recovery helicopter is the one that recovered the Apollo 8 and Apollo 10 astronauts. An intensely proud moment this for the crew of Helicopter 66.

David Brinkley @BNBCNews
Well, you can't say the navy is not ecumenical. The ship's band is playing the air force song as the chopper is being winched forward along the deck.

David Brinkley @BNBCNews
The commander, Neil Armstrong, is a former navy man of course. But the other two crew members are air force service members.

David Brinkley @BNBCNews
As soon as the helicopter landed, a chief ran out and stuck a symbol of a spacecraft on the nose of the

chopper. It now proudly displays the symbols of 3 spacecrafts: Apollo 8, Apollo 10 and Apollo 11.

Chet Huntley @CHNBCNews
President Nixon watching intently from the admiral's bridge seems genuinely moved by this moment. And who could fail to be moved by such moments?

David Brinkley @BNBCNews
The helicopter with the astronauts still inside is on the elevator and is now descending to the hanger deck where they will disembark and go immediately into the mobile quarantine facility.

David Brinkley @BNBCNews
A tractor is now hauling number 66 helicopter inboard off of number 2 elevator. The president has now left the bridge being followed by a gaggle of reporters and cameramen.

Chet Huntley @CHNBCNews
We see the astronauts emerging from the helicopter now wearing their special protective garments and large gas masks, or respirators if you prefer.

Chet Huntley @CHNBCNews
Just one brief wave to the cheering sailors and newsmen.

*The Apollo 11 astronauts leaving helicopter 66
onboard USS Hornet*

Chet Huntley @CHNBCNews
Now the astronauts briskly enter the waiting mobile
quarantine facility and the door is closed.

David Brinkley @BNBCNews
The steps which the astronauts used to depart the helicopter are now being sprayed with butyraldehyde, a decontaminant solution – one of the many NASA procedures designed to prevent contamination by any lunar viruses brought back by the astronauts.

Chet Huntley @CHNBCNews
The presidential seal has now been attached to the door of the mobile quarantine facility as we await the appearance of the president.

David Brinkley @BNBCNews
As the ship's band plays "Hail to the Chief", here comes the president onto the hanger deck where the mobile quarantine facility with the astronauts inside is located.

David Brinkley @BNBCNews
Smiling broadly, the president walks up to and stands in front of the facility door and its viewing window. As he does so, the astronauts immediately pull back the curtains and we see the faces of three very happy young men.

Richard M. Nixon @RMNUSPresident
I think I am the luckiest man in the world. Not just
because I am the president, but because I have the
privilege of speaking for so many in welcoming these
men back to Earth.

Richard M. Nixon @RMNUSPresident
Over 100 foreign countries, presidents, prime
ministers and kings, representing over 2 billion people
on this planet, have sent the most warm messages
that we have ever received.

Richard M. Nixon @RMNUSPresident
Yesterday, I called three of the most gracious ladies I
know - the wives of the astronauts. Unlike my call to
the Moon, I did not make those calls collect the
astronauts will be happy to hear.

Richard M. Nixon @RMNUSPresident
I have a little secret to confess. I made a date with all
three of those ladies. I invited them to dinner on the
13th. August, right after their husbands come out of
quarantine.

Richard M. Nixon @RMNUSPresident
It will be a state dinner, held in Los Angeles. The
governors of all 50 states will be there, as well as
ambassadors from all around the world. NASA told me
there is a good chance the three husbands will come
too.

Neil Armstrong @CMDRApollo11
We surely do appreciate the invitation and we will do
anything, go anywhere, the president says.

Richard M. Nixon @RMNUSPresident
Boy, those three astronauts look great! Frank Borman says according to Dr. Einstein's theory, they are a little younger by reason of going into space. Is that right? I wonder if they feel a little younger.

Michael Collins @CMPApollo11
Well, we're all a lot younger than Frank Borman. Almost everybody is.

Richard M. Nixon @RMNUSPresident
Here comes Frank Borman to have a word with the crew. I don't think he's going to take that last comment lying down.

Frank Borman @FBApollo8
You know, we have a supposed poet in Mike Collins and he really gave me a hard time after my Apollo 8

mission for using words like "fantastic" and "beautiful" so often.

Frank Borman @FBApollo8
I listened to Mike's comments from space, and during just one three-minute period he used 4 fantastics and 3 beautifuls. Not so good for a so-called poet.

Walter Cronkite @WCCBSNews
These astronauts love to rib each other, but we all know the deep, deep sense of brotherhood each one of them feels for the others.

Richard M. Nixon @RMNUSPresident
This mission has lasted just over a week, but it has been the greatest week in the history of the world since the Creation.

Richard M. Nixon @RMNUSPresident
As a result of what happened this week, the world is bigger – infinitely. As a result of what these men have done, the world has never been closer together.

Richard M. Nixon @RMNUSPresident
We thank them for that, and I only hope that all of us in government, all of us in America, that as a result of what they have done, we can do our job a little better – that we can reach for the stars just as these men have done.

Richard M. Nixon @RMNUSPresident
I reminded the astronauts that if they make any speeches at the state dinner, people prefer short speeches and that if they want to say "fantastic" and "beautiful", that's fine with me.

David Brinkley @BNBCNews
And now, the astronauts, the president and everyone on the hanger deck stand to attention as the navy band plays the Star-Spangled Banner.

David Brinkley @BNBCNews
The president is now leaving to embark on his trip around the world. The Hornet will sail to Honolulu and from there, the astronauts in their sealed container will be flown to Houston.

David Brinkley @BNBCNews
In Houston, a somewhat roomier quarantine building awaits them. So far, there is no evidence of any infection or any unwholesome effects from the Moon.

David Brinkley @BNBCNews
If it turns out, as everyone expects, that there won't be any harmful effects as a result of this mission, then it will have been a rarity in human affairs – a total success.

Jules Bergman @JBABC News
President John F. Kennedy laid out the goal saying we had to put a man on the Moon and bring him safely back to Earth by 1970 and we have.

Jules Bergman @JBABC News
And now Apollo 12 lies ahead... a new landing site, a new goal. New dangers as well as new rewards. Then Apollo 13, 14 and 15 next year.

David Brinkley @BNBCNews
To say, as we now can, that somebody has landed on the Moon and walked around on it, while almost everybody on Earth watched, is just about too much to swallow. I almost don't even believe it.

David Brinkley @BNBCNews
But it's true. Men did land and walk on the Moon. And if this is not a permanent, enduring event in human history, then nothing is. This momentous event will be remembered as long as mankind remembers anything.

The massive tickertape parade through New York City following the successful Apollo 11 mission.

The End

Thank you so much for reading #Houston69. I hope you enjoyed reading it as much as I enjoyed researching and writing it. If you did enjoy the book and have the time and inclination, please consider leaving a review on the book's page at Amazon.

If you enjoyed this book, you may also enjoy my follow-on book: **#Houston70: The Miracle Journey of Apollo 13.**

There are several other Hashtag Histories books currently available. To see them, or to sign up for notifications of new releases, please visit my website at: www.hashtaghistories.com

Major Sources

Timelines, NASA documents, astronaut accounts, etc.

NASA air to ground transcripts
https://www.hq.nasa.gov/alsj/a11/a11transcript_tec.pdf

NASA PAO commentary
http://www.jsc.nasa.gov/history/mission_trans/AS11_PAO.PDF

NEIL ARMSTRONG – A RARE INTERVIEW 2011
https://www.youtube.com/watch?v=t57KgcnQQaQ
If you watch none of the other footage in my sources of before, during and after the Apollo 11 mission, watch this one! I highly recommend it.

http://history.nasa.gov/SP-4029/Apollo_11i_Timeline.htm

http://www.space.com/26558-apollo-11-anniversary-complete-coverage.html

Apollo 11: Mission Overview: Lunar and Planetary Institute
http://www.lpi.usra.edu/lunar/missions/apollo/apollo_11/overview/

Apollo 11 Flight Journal
http://history.nasa.gov/ap11fj/index.htm

You Tube: Apollo 11: The untold Story.
https://www.youtube.com/watch?v=wYzvVjRtn5Y

Live TV News coverage from CBS, NBC and ABC Television Networks (104 Broadcasts over 8 days)

PRE LAUNCH

https://www.youtube.com/watch?v=x6m1TU-i4yY&index=2&list=PLwxFr1zAEfokQUXPUyyss0qp1Unqax5AU

https://www.youtube.com/watch?v=g_Ay9x0_hzA&index=3&list=PLwxFr1zAEfokQUXPUyyss0qp1Unqax5AU

https://www.youtube.com/watch?v=v25zdUcDvZg&list=PLwxFr1zAEfokQUXPUyyss0qp1Unqax5AU&index=4

https://www.youtube.com/watch?v=IyVBHArDJz0&index=5&list=PLwxFr1zAEfokQUXPUyyss0qp1Unqax5AU

RUN UP TO LAUNCH

https://www.youtube.com/watch?v=3mjSosOV_Mk&index=6&list=PLwxFr1zAEfokQUXPUyyss0qp1Unqax5AU

https://www.youtube.com/watch?v=L-ozBhmXCq4&list=PLwxFr1zAEfokQUXPUyyss0qp1Unqax5AU&index=7

https://www.youtube.com/watch?v=Kiy2sipD9MA&list=PLwxFr1zAEfokQUXPUyyss0qp1Unqax5AU&index=8

https://www.youtube.com/watch?v=TPLwxFr1zAEfokQUXPUyyss0qp1Unqax5AU&index=9

https://www.youtube.com/watch?v=IyY9oAYkd98&list=PLwxFr1zAEfokQUXPUyyss0qp1Unqax5AU&index=10

https://www.youtube.com/watch?v=P1QO1ZIuSrI&list=PLwxFr1zAEfokQUXPUyyss0qp1Unqax5AU&index=11

COUNTDOWN AND LAUNCH

https://www.youtube.com/watch?v=wEjGe6XmO9U&list=PLwxFr1zAEfokQUXPUyyss0qp1Unqax5AU&index=18

https://www.youtube.com/watch?v=yDhcYhrCPmc&list=PLwxFr1zAEfokQUXPUyyss0qp1Unqax5AU&index=17

https://www.youtube.com/watch?v=JxohAQPwE4s&index=12&list=PLwxFr1zAEfokQUXPUyyss0qp1Unqax5AU

https://www.youtube.com/watch?v=wEjGe6XmO9U&list=PLwxFr1zAEfokQUXPUyyss0qp1Unqax5AU&index=18

https://www.youtube.com/watch?v=FQ8TfjWHsGQ&list=PLwxFr1zAEfokQUXPUyyss0qp1Unqax5AU&index=19

https://www.youtube.com/watch?v=WYBsEq6prHE&list=PLwxFr1zAEfokQUXPUyyss0qp1Unqax5AU&index=20

https://www.youtube.com/watch?v=mBvYptZmi2s&list=PLwxFr1zAEfokQUXPUyyss0qp1Unqax5AU&index=13

https://www.youtube.com/watch?v=EynafZoK_A8&index=14&list=PLwxFr1zAEfokQUXPUyyss0qp1Unqax5AU

https://www.youtube.com/watch?v=vRhgnYQBZvU&list=PLwxFr1zAEfokQUXPUyyss0qp1Unqax5AU&index=15

https://www.youtube.com/watch?v=hRFoeAgkZSg&index=16&list=PLwxFr1zAEfokQUXPUyyss0qp1Unqax5AU

https://www.youtube.com/watch?v=U9WEZMCLwnc&index=23&list=PLwxFr1zAEfokQUXPUyyss0qp1Unqax5AU

https://www.youtube.com/watch?v=vcvcLSpfQYM&list=PLwxFr1zAEfokQUXPUyyss0qp1Unqax5AU&index=24

https://www.youtube.com/watch?v=RcP66XB9yxA&list=PLwxFr1zAEfokQUXPUyyss0qp1Unqax5AU&index=25

TO THE MOON

https://www.youtube.com/watch?v=CdgV4o_KLpc&index=26&list=PLwxFr1zAEfokQUXPUyyss0qp1Unqax5AU

https://www.youtube.com/watch?v=viAdtsjAjdY&index=27&list=PLwxFr1zAEfokQUXPUyyss0qp1Unqax5AU

https://www.youtube.com/watch?v=XjvN135-hwU&list=PLwxFr1zAEfokQUXPUyyss0qp1Unqax5AU&index=38

https://www.youtube.com/watch?v=sU5sFob5vlI&list=PLwxFr1zAEfokQUXPUyyss0qp1Unqax5AU&index=39

https://www.youtube.com/watch?v=wbMXqu2PBH4&index=40&list=PLwxFr1zAEfokQUXPUyyss0qp1Unqax5AU

https://www.youtube.com/watch?v=LOt0t1Zv9JE&list=PLwxFr1zAEfokQUXPUyyss0qp1Unqax5AU&index=41

https://www.youtube.com/watch?v=4UeL-acj-8k&list=PLwxFr1zAEfokQUXPUyyss0qp1Unqax5AU&index=42

https://www.youtube.com/watch?v=SoIvSbdPlQs&list=PLwxFr1zAEfokQUXPUyyss0qp1Unqax5AU&index=43

https://www.youtube.com/watch?v=vhAKZ_5_LJo&list=PLwxFr1zAEfokQUXPUyyss0qp1Unqax5AU&index=44

https://www.youtube.com/watch?v=5vLYnBTucOs&index=45&list=PLwxFr1zAEfokQUXPUyyss0qp1Unqax5AU

https://www.youtube.com/watch?v=YlSGo8bI6QI&index=46&list=PLwxFr1zAEfokQUXPUyyss0qp1Unqax5AU

https://www.youtube.com/watch?v=BwZMKALHLHk&list=PLwxFr1zAEfokQUXPUyyss0qp1Unqax5AU&index=49

https://www.youtube.com/watch?v=gM6NPuagKow&index=50&list=PLwxFr1zAEfokQUXPUyyss0qp1Unqax5AU

https://www.youtube.com/watch?v=0s91KF6gKQE&list=PLwxFr1zAEfokQUXPUyyss0qp1Unqax5AU&index=51

THE LANDING ON THE MOON

https://www.youtube.com/watch?v=K0ZiVl9K6bg&index=52&list=PLwxFr1zAEfokQUXPUyyss0qp1Unqax5AU

https://www.youtube.com/watch?v=eoy8IWjwb1k&list=PLwxFr1zAEfokQUXPUyyss0qp1Unqax5AU&index=53

https://www.youtube.com/watch?v=l1AzFcsHS_w&index=55&list=PLwxFr1zAEfokQUXPUyyss0qp1Unqax5AU

https://www.youtube.com/watch?v=9ojFAea0nGI&index=54&list=PLwxFr1zAEfokQUXPUyyss0qp1Unqax5AU

https://www.youtube.com/watch?v=3xMV6mIi8tE&list=PLwxFr1zAEfokQUXPUyyss0qp1Unqax5AU&index=56

https://www.youtube.com/watch?v=fZJbynzj2j4&list=PLwxFr1zAEfokQUXPUyyss0qp1Unqax5AU&index=57

https://www.youtube.com/watch?v=3JRK1HBHKrM&list=PLwxFr1zAEfokQUXPUyyss0qp1Unqax5AU&index=58

THE MOONWALK AND SCIENTIFIC EXPERIMENTS

https://www.youtube.com/watch?v=XisDvCTww4M&index=59&list=PLwxFr1zAEfokQUXPUyyss0qp1Unqax5AU

https://www.youtube.com/watch?v=F24PE1fYDMg&list=PLwxFr1zAEfokQUXPUyyss0qp1Unqax5AU&index=70

https://www.youtube.com/watch?v=8F99kkxmIjk&index=60&list=PLwxFr1zAEfokQUXPUyyss0qp1Unqax5AU

https://www.youtube.com/watch?v=oqujCUoCz8M&list=PLwxFr1zAEfokQUXPUyyss0qp1Unqax5AU&index=82

https://www.youtube.com/watch?v=nnaJyWMn30k&list=PLwxFr1zAEfokQUXPUyyss0qp1Unqax5AU&index=61

https://www.youtube.com/watch?v=sEfwtZSiGwA&list=PLwxFr1zAEfokQUXPUyyss0qp1Unqax5AU&index=72

https://www.youtube.com/watch?v=HvfqMmvx2vk&index=62&list=PLwxFr1zAEfokQUXPUyyss0qp1Unqax5AU

https://www.youtube.com/watch?v=Ifts6zZw1JE&list=PLwxFr1zAEfokQUXPUyyss0qp1Unqax5AU&index=83

https://www.youtube.com/watch?v=qhx2UUzbCyM&list=PLwxFr1zAEfokQUXPUyyss0qp1Unqax5AU&index=73

https://www.youtube.com/watch?v=mqsQi7UW3H0&list=PLwxFr1zAEfokQUXPUyyss0qp1Unqax5AU&index=74

https://www.youtube.com/watch?v=dxl7ndDJWgM&index=84&list=PLwxFr1zAEfokQUXPUyyss0qp1Unqax5AU

https://www.youtube.com/watch?v=rUbf0SC0BW8&list=PLwxFr1zAEfokQUXPUyyss0qp1Unqax5AU&index=63

https://www.youtube.com/watch?v=Lv4Z23Nxku4&list=PLwxFr1zAEfokQUXPUyyss0qp1Unqax5AU&index=75

https://www.youtube.com/watch?v=gZDZEU-sFYw&index=64&list=PLwxFr1zAEfokQUXPUyyss0qp1Unqax5AU

https://www.youtube.com/watch?v=GiuypC4mKIA&index=76&list=PLwxFr1zAEfokQUXPUyyss0qp1Unqax5AU

https://www.youtube.com/watch?v=5S_bYHczEjg&list=PLwxFr1zAEfokQUXPUyyss0qp1Unqax5AU&index=77

https://www.youtube.com/watch?v=Bc76A2Z_FYo&index=65&list=PLwxFr1zAEfokQUXPUyyss0qp1Unqax5AU

https://www.youtube.com/watch?v=RiGngF5T3TM&index=79&list=PLwxFr1zAEfokQUXPUyyss0qp1Unqax5AU

https://www.youtube.com/watch?v=RiGngF5T3TM&index=79&list=PLwxFr1zAEfokQUXPUyyss0qp1Unqax5AU

https://www.youtube.com/watch?v=5tLOy-GBtjE&index=67&list=PLwxFr1zAEfokQUXPUyyss0qp1Unqax5AU

THE JOURNEY HOME

https://www.youtube.com/watch?v=Q6raBLm-454&list=PLwxFr1zAEfokQUXPUyyss0qp1Unqax5AU&index=68

https://www.youtube.com/watch?v=8dTjUvu1hIU&index=85&list=PLwxFr1zAEfokQUXPUyyss0qp1Unqax5AU

https://www.youtube.com/watch?v=0cgaKWU3g-g&list=PLwxFr1zAEfokQUXPUyyss0qp1Unqax5AU&index=86

https://www.youtube.com/watch?v=Dqlq1gzP5bw&list=PLwxFr1zAEfokQUXPUyyss0qp1Unqax5AU&index=81

https://www.youtube.com/watch?v=k61BBOenOPY&index=69&list=PLwxFr1zAEfokQUXPUyyss0qp1Unqax5AU

https://www.youtube.com/watch?v=0cgaKWU3g-g&list=PLwxFr1zAEfokQUXPUyyss0qp1Unqax5AU&index=86

https://www.youtube.com/watch?v=yY6BySTwkvE&list=PLwxFr1zAEfokQUXPUyyss0qp1Unqax5AU&index=87

https://www.youtube.com/watch?v=46CxBQJ9860&list=PLwxFr1zAEfokQUXPUyyss0qp1Unqax5AU&index=88

https://www.youtube.com/watch?v=b2KxSIsr6oo&list=PLwxFr1zAEfokQUXPUyyss0qp1Unqax5AU&index=91

https://www.youtube.com/watch?v=NzksT5HvLB8&list=PLwxFr1zAEfokQUXPUyyss0qp1Unqax5AU&index=92

https://www.youtube.com/watch?v=TM1jpfABQvo&index=93&list=PLwxFr1zAEfokQUXPUyyss0qp1Unqax5AU

https://www.youtube.com/watch?v=9RDHkmpiIRo&list=PLwxFr1zAEfokQUXPUyyss0qp1Unqax5AU&index=94

https://www.youtube.com/watch?v=BM_5As7g79E&list=PLwxFr1zAEfokQUXPUyyss0qp1Unqax5AU&index=89

https://www.youtube.com/watch?v=MCXXcI6YyBc&index=90&list=PLwxFr1zAEfokQUXPUyyss0qp1Unqax5AU

RE-ENTRY AND RECOVERY

https://www.youtube.com/watch?v=9RDHkmpiIRo&list=PLwxFr1zAEfokQUXPUyyss0qp1Unqax5AU&index=94

https://www.youtube.com/watch?v=QtwSJ_GjUmw&list=PLwxFr1zAEfokQUXPUyyss0qp1Unqax5AU&index=95

https://www.youtube.com/watch?v=CKcPg_--bCc&index=96&list=PLwxFr1zAEfokQUXPUyyss0qp1Unqax5AU

https://www.youtube.com/playlist?list=PLwxFr1zAEfokQUXPUyyss0qp1Unqax5AU

https://www.youtube.com/watch?v=yDhcYhrCPmc&list=PLwxFr1zAEfokQUXPUyyss0qp1Unqax5AU&index=18

https://www.youtube.com/watch?v=jU0B-loHHTM&index=97&list=PLwxFr1zAEfokQUXPUyyss0qp1Unqax5AU

https://www.youtube.com/watch?v=1LEDkzdjZkA&list=PLwxFr1zAEfokQUXPUyyss0qp1Unqax5AU&index=98

Recommended Reading

Magnificent Desolation: The Long Journey Home from the Moon by Buzz Aldrin and Ken Abraham. ISBN: 978-0307463463

Carrying the Fire by Michael Collins. ISBN-10: 0374531943

Failure is not an Option by Gene Kranz. ISBN: 0743200799

Moonfire by Norman Mailer ISBN: 383652077X

Return to Earth by Edwin E Aldrin and Wayne Warga. ISBN: 978-0394488325

A Man on the Moon by Andrew Chaikin. ISBN: 014311235X

Next:

#Houston68

Apollo 8 – The Longest Journey

And:

#Houston 70
The Miracle Journey of Apollo 13

Printed in Great Britain
by Amazon